THE CONSCIOUSNESS OF MAN

REGINALD O'NEAL GIBSON

THE CONSCIOUSNESS OF MAN

REGINALD O'NEAL GIBSON
Copyright © 2016 Reginald Gibson

ISBN-13: 978-0692610527

ISBN: 0692610529

Printed in the United States

All rights reserved. No part of this publication may be reproduced, distributed, or transmitted in any form or by any means, including photocopying, recording, or other electronic or mechanical methods, without the prior written permission of the publisher, except in the case of brief quotations embodied in critical reviews and certain other noncommercial uses permitted by copyright law. For permission requests, write to the publisher, addressed "Attention: Permissions Coordinator," at chefreginald@gmail.com and or zoeylifesite.com

REGINALD O'NEAL GIBSON

DEDICATION

I dedicate this book to my wife, Kelly Lynn Gibson. She has flourished within the light of the Holy Spirit and has surely fulfilled the covenant God created within her heart. By the brilliance of her smile and the softness of her touch, I've overcome barriers and have emerged as the "leader by example," which God instilled deeply within my spirit. I couldn't have become any happier, that is until she gave birth to our triplets, Gabriel, Adalynn, and Christian.

Thank you, Kelly.

REGINALD O'NEAL GIBSON

THE COMMITMENT

What's on your heart? _____

_____

Who are you at this point of your life? _____

_____

Are you willing to enhance your life as well as the lives of people around you? _____

Do you commit to becoming free of the bondages, stressors and negative emotions, that could hold you back from a life of complete happiness and abundance? _____

Date _____/ _____/ _____

I believe in you, I have faith in you and I dedicate prayer, love, and peace towards the commitment of your journey. God bless.

REGINALD O'NEAL GIBSON

Contents

1. Temperament of the Seed .... pg. 13

2. The Turning Point .... pg. 31

3. In the Bosom of the Holy Spirit .... pg. 49

4. Against the Grain .... pg. 61

5. Let's Talk About It .... pg. 75

6. The Pulse of the Mountain .... pg. 109

7. The Awakening .... pg. 117

8. Journey through the Darkness .... pg. 133

9. The Light of the World .... pg. 141

10. The Transparency of a Novice .... pg. 151

11. Travelers Amongst Us .... pg. 163

12. The Perspective .... pg. 183

REGINALD O'NEAL GIBSON

Acknowledgments

We've found each other once again, only this time it's in the physical realm. Please do not dismiss the content of this book as merely chance, coincidence, or even curiosity. The task has fallen upon myself to fulfill our agreement by calling to action all who have been exposed to a higher consciousness. Emerge from your worldly image, break free of the perception of mental bondage, and stand deeply rooted within the soil of your purpose. We have been chosen and endowed with a blessed responsibility, not a burden. Come back to the clarity of your mind and remember we are as one on this journey. I ask that you unveil the truth in your creation and give rise to a higher essence in life. This reveals a truth in knowledge, unfolding as the unfathomable wisdom within the subconsciousness of your mind. It is meant to be, shall be once again, and is now; forevermore. Awaken, my friends, as the higher humans ushering in humanity's next level of consciousness.

REGINALD O'NEAL GIBSON

Chapter 1

Temperament of the Seed

As a child, I found life a never-ending adventure; like many children, I was always running, jumping, climbing trees, and of course falling down more times than I could possibly remember. This was of great importance, for this was the beginning of the unconditional will needed for training. Pursuing truth and honoring focused decision-making, even after failed attempts, were acts of valor, purpose-driven pride, and courage. This was the echoing of my heart.

If ever I found myself in despair after a failure, I'd absorb the internal affirmations I needed to push forward and continuously uncover ways to save the world. I remember the daunting realms revealed to justify and balance those echoing words, which by then had saturated my mind. It was a small voice, whispering quietly as if to keep a secret, repeating over and over again, "Get up, Reggie—you have something to do."

Naturally accepting the role of a knight in shining armor, I found myself continuously preparing for the battle, preparing to one day save my princess, my purpose, and then the world. The zeal of my passion seemed to flow effortlessly as I conquered swinging from branches and hurdling fences. My boldness was unchallenged as I played in my backyard, while wielding a garbage can top as my shield of justice.

No one would dare question my path of becoming a true superhero, a warrior for no other reason than to protect all that is good. I was always filled with anticipation and wonder, but this is normal for those in their youth. Although many times I questioned myself, "Am I any different from others my age?" *Not likely,* comforted my mind—I had this gut feeling others were training as well. I knew that when we finally met, I was going to be ready to join and march with the victors of enlightenment.

So on I went, throughout the better part of my days doing battle with all that opposed my perceptions, honor, or will—that is, until I crossed paths with an unlikely foe. Equally determined in his instinctual purpose, our worlds inevitably collide, and this marked one of my first tests.

Not to be clichéd, but as with most stories of fate, it all began on a particularly sunny day. While walking to my destination, I soon found myself running from my neighbor's dog. No sweat at all—I was fast—but on this day, he was just a bit faster. Again, no worries; aside from basking in the glory of my training, I also excelled as a diplomat. Soon after, Cuddles and I came to an agreement of respective understanding: First, that no one would run across his yard. Second, that he could basically run in any yard he pleased, granted he was temporarily off his chain.

Okay, it was not much of a victory on my behalf, but it turned out fine nonetheless, especially since the miniature Doberman pinscher never chased anyone who walked in a controlled manner past his domain.

THE CONSCIOUSNESS OF MAN

It may have appeared odd to people, but Cuddles and I often found ourselves locked in a fierce game of who would move first, while gazing beyond the gaps in the fence. However, what people thought was of no concern, for we knew that when the need arose, we would be the ones more than prepared to defend our homes.

Moreover, confident in my ways, I presumed I had a firm understanding on my limitations, courtesy of my past failures, blunders, and embarrassments. But that didn't stop me from pushing onward to my next challenge. Life as we know it often finds ways of throwing a curve when you least expect it. My curve in this thing called life was the absence of the tangible figure of the formidable foe that I'd come to expect. This thing, this entity, was without form, so apprehensively I found myself digesting the question, *How can I do battle with such a force?* It was not as if I could take hold of its legs with rope or even pull out my shield of justice to deflect its fiery flames.

I was at a loss, but if I could only pierce its armor-like scales to penetrate its heart of dark purpose, then all would be well. Humbled in my beginnings, I found out the phrase "Life is a beast" was a gross understatement, being that its concept was far greater than any mythical monster any man could conjure up. I've found that in some instances, those seeking power create false enemies for the purposes of invoking fear and superstition amongst the masses. This perpetuates their lust for power, as they continually seek to spew misguided ideas for personal gain.

Those attempting to lead this way only find that manifestations of their apathy will quickly guarantee a yield of empty followers. Even with the acknowledgment of this truth, it sheds light on the fact that, when man finally reaches maturity, the stories of overcoming evil are twofold at best. On one side are courage and valor, and on the other is man's false dominion over woman and the Earth, but that's a story for another day.

Even still, the question remains: How could I wage my battle of purpose against the vast entity of life, without doubt the most powerful of all forces, though not a physical foe? And yet I continuously felt an overwhelming sense of peace still whispering words of truth into my spirit. This manifested awareness, this hidden secret would one day uncover a power that could mold the reality of life as I saw fit. I was only seven years old, but I was consumed with responsibility and focus. The weight of the world was on my heart. But what could I say? That echoing was still there, only now it was speaking a bit louder: "Get up, Reggie—you have something to do!"

This battle of the mind wasn't just my battle, even though many times I felt alone; it was shared with hundreds of thousands of people, young and old, across the world, each with their own distinct purpose as well. We only needed to find each other in order to continuously sway the balance toward good. Although it appeared to be an impossible task to communicate and share each other's stories or advices, we often had communion at the gates within the spirit world.

Many children just like myself traveled under the cloak of dreams, imagination, and nightmares; this is an essential part of calculated formations, for this strengthened us without our knowing we were in training. Some of us were great speakers in the spirit world, and we've carried great influence with us, with the ability to talk so that all forms of doubt, pain, or insecurity would leave upon the vibration of our voices. Others' spirits were leaders by example, yielding the powers of confidence and destroying any form of doubts or fears; these leaders possessed the ability to inspire and change the minds of the multitudes simply by walking in the presence of truth and authority.

Lastly, I recall spirits with the powers of health, playfully flying around, defying what we know on earth as gravity. These were the spirits that, within their surroundings, healed the anointed who were tired and burdened; their light was a shimmering glow, nurturing all that came into contact with the warmth of its aura. Seems far-fetched according to the perceptions of the world today; you might assume these are just fables meant to occupy the mind in the forms of fairy tales and bedtime stories, but have you ever asked yourself why? Why would people create such visions?

Why would people share stories such as these when we're already living in such a confusing world? We the storytellers don't share for personal gain or for selfishness. We share with the hope of allowing the possibility of truth to resonate in the minds of our listeners. Sharing our stories sets the foundation, and one day we'll stand upon these visions as the solidification of truth as it comes to pass.

Know that every building or structure we look upon, dwelled in or acknowledge to be magnificent on this planet, was once a thought embedded by an idea. Ushered in by way of a vision or dream; in this imagination was the vessel that nurtured the seed of mankind's will. Yet still the question remains, why do we share these stories? Why since the dawn of time have our ancestors thought it vital to pass down these impressions and visions set within our spirits? My answer to this comes from a source I'll get into a little later in the book, but for now I'll answer the question by posing another question: Are you actually living in a world that's as harsh as you've come to believe or have you fallen victim, to the persuasions and idealistic nature of a stronghold's belief system?

What if I told you that the reason it is suggested that we only use 10 percent of our brains' capacity, is to keep us from having focused awareness and living up to our fullest potential? In this enlightenment, allowing for the possibility of a mind shift or paradigm change to reveal that our reality is just a multitude of thoughts, suggestions, and visions, opening to sensations indicative of what we've come to know as dreams. So, I pose the questions: What have you come to know as a dream? Is it a memory, thought process or for that matter even real? How do you know?

Think about it: Was yesterday, last week, or three years ago a dream? Have you ever thought, "Did I actually do that or was it a dream from my past?" Clearly what you did yesterday can only be recollected by way of thought, memory, or images bringing about manifested sensations.

What if I told you that if you accept this into your reality, then the other 90 percent of our being is on the other side. Furthermore, battling within the spirit world as to compensate for not fully embracing our strengths here? Maybe we're just visiting here on an as-needed basis but an important basis of balance nonetheless. In other words, consider your world as you see it now just a dream or training grounds for your true spiritual and developmental journey. Now what if I said that more power is needed here, to gain the power of salvation there? Maybe this is why a sacrificer allowed himself to be crucified, willingly died then rose again to give us the ability to be awakened. Moreover, if accepted, gives us the blessed ability to be free from burdened and conscious clarified from the wiles of deception lurking in this world.

Ponder this, our bodies need rest to heal; we fall asleep at night not because we want to but to physically recharge and to achieve physiological homeostasis. Maybe we are consciously here in sleep to utilize the time to become spiritually molded and to prepare for the eternity of our souls. Let's consider what happens in this reality and remember we're all in training, as I related in the start to my story. On earth we carry incredible powers, but many have fallen prey to the idea that we are powerless, yielding large percentages of our minds to be controlled, leaving only dormancy, confusion, and despair.

This is partially due to allowing those running the principalities and strongholds of this world to use heterosuggestions, misinformation, and fear to form barriers within our thought processes—in other words to manipulate the minds of many, developing false perceptions and clouded mind-sets.

A person thus taken over soon becomes a void shell of a temple, which is nothing more than an empty follower for purposes of the devourer.

Too fast or far-fetched? Okay, maybe you're not a part of such an insidious process, but let's look deeper into this understanding. I used the word *heterosuggestions*, meaning suggestions meant to influence your mind, and then the word *manipulate*, meaning to sway or alter by persuasion. This means a created void in the mind, making it ready to submit to the will of other forces. Is this starting to sound more feasible? I'm not pointing fingers or trying to pick on specific advertisers, law makers or politicians, especially around voting season but seriously, ask yourself, what or who controls your mind? Have you developed an opinion about a certain someone or subject matter based solely off the representation of the perceived powers that be?

What has made up or contributed to your thought process before actually making up your mind in times of important decisions? Remember, saturation of truth is needed to bring forth the possibility of an enlightened yield. Upon this harvest, we will have produced a field of newfound knowledge, so let's slow down a bit because the opposite, that is the saturation of miseducation or blatant lies can also lead, but only to yields of negativity, which are not good for our created purposes. We were just questioning the impact or idea of rest and dreams, which personally I've come to know as a spiritual covenant. With this said, let's touch back on dreams.

Consider your brain a vessel within a dream-like state, which creates or persuades your own versions or embedded perceptions of life. What if I said that when you fall asleep *here*, you wake up *there*, losing most memories within the travel? What if I said the role you choose in this realm vastly affects the battle that goes on in the spirit realm? This is why it's so vital to take back the consciousness of your mind; here, in this reality! It's imperative not to inadvertently give control of your mind to other forces, who will interact on your behalf elsewhere. However, don't let this induce stress upon your heart, being as we do have help from time to time, which is why I spoke of the three kinds of spirits meeting at the gates earlier.

Here's a hint, the spirits will interact upon the battlefield of the mind. The only issue is you must cleanse your mind in such a way that no doubts exist, meaning you'll need to start all over again, if distracted by trying to figure out the world you live in now. Think of it like hitting "system restore" on your computer that's been taken over by a virus, wiping the slate completely clean. Being stuck in doubt, trying to make since of all the lies and misguided ways of this world could explain why so many people repeatedly tread through the same issues in life, struggling in a paradigm of the depressed or mundane.

Also let me add, if you're willing to accept the possibility of this being true, it requires that you confirm it for yourself. Here's what you need to do: stay focused and follow the many principles of peace, sacrifice, and commitment, while enduring the hardships of this world to properly prepare you for the battle within the mind. Throughout this book there will be hints, analogies, and self-help processes to get you there.

Also, don't forget the veritable plethora of Bible's, doctrines, and positive influences made available by others, all within your reach. Of course, there are many other spirits and forms of righteousness within and around our environment, but I haven't had the pleasure of communion by way of visions or dreams just yet. Also, since this book is not fictional, I'm convicted to share only my experiences, dreams, and spiritual awakenings.

Yes, I include dreams as "truthful," being as I've developed the understanding of a dream's purpose. They are not what we've been taught they are. Let's compare them to the imagination. Up until now, most have chosen to imagine with the tools, visions, and suggestions of this world, diminishing their creative limits to minuscule at best. What if I suggested that your imagination is like the alphabet? I might remind you that there are hundreds more than the twenty-six letters we were taught? Most would say that's common sense, but if so, why is our communication as a people so uncommonly inferior?

Is it the implanted limitations within our minds or the reflected vulnerability of forgotten knowledge? Consider this: there are sounds, vibrations, words, and feelings needed to unlock secrets, open minds, and positively manipulate the physical realm. Most will never access these because they've settled for just the right amount of knowledge to keep them content—again, twenty-six letters. So, as previously stated, I've developed an understanding as to what dreams really are and what their true purpose is for our lives. My best explanation will be described through an analogy, being that it's more of an understanding than a point.

When I speak to you face-to-face, my voice box resonates with vibrations that are manipulated by my larynx, mouth, and lips. Simultaneously, a visualization or thought process is developed in both our minds. It's articulated and construed in the form of energy, beginning its journey across space or the mass between our bodies. On my side there is a picture produced on the canvas of my mind being transmitted, reflected or shared to the unconscious state of your mind. Only when you view this canvas, the weight of your consciousness fills in the gaps if any with fears or opinions based from unclarified reasoning.

This is to say, when the vessel of your mind receives it, it's absorbed within your consciousness. How you interpret my energy is solely based upon your embedded perceptions, resulting in your comprehension. So, consider dreams to be a form of energy or signal, channeling through your mind as bridges between realms. This can be done with absolute clarity, if the mind is still and void of distractions. Know that if there is any obstacle between the channels, comprehension can be obstructed, clouded, and terribly impaired. This is the lure of nightmares and fantasies, not from a realm of clairvoyance and truth but rather your desires or fears mucking the channels of communications. It's like when you're at a concert, and you have to yell at your friends for them to understand you—and they still may not get the message.

The space between our bodies is now cluttered with other intentions and vibrations, and this leads to confusion and clouded perceptions.

Don't believe me? Why does the majority of the population turn down the music in the car in preparation to parallel park? The answer is, the communicative concentration needed from your eyes to signal your brain that it's safe to park. This stimulates an immediate chain reaction of equilibrium, stabilization, and coordination needed to perform the necessary motor skills: clicking the turn signal, reversing the wheel, applying pressure to the gas and then brakes. You must do all this while chewing gum, checking your mirror, and screaming at the kids to be quiet. All this to provide a coordinated expression of physical understanding.

Again, in the absence of clarity, the mind tries to fill the gaps in communication with assumptions and probabilities. This leads to unrest, physically and spiritually; in other words, things simply don't add up—kind of like a dream, right? Remember, your dreams are a place where your brain will plug in fears, worries, and often stressors from the days leading up to now, when your actual intention is to recuperate physically through rest. This is one of the reasons why I removed the television from my bedroom, and I strive not to go to sleep reviewing all the problematic issues, concerns, or stressors I encountered throughout that day. Your mind is like an antenna, delivering and receiving information between worlds. The only issue is that the radio station that is your brain is bombarded and overstimulated by thousands of other transmitting antennas. Learning to create clarity of communication prevents the dissolution and clutter hindering your focus while this two-way channel is open.

Dreams are the sum total of your faith, insecurities, and embedded fears, as well as inspirations and memories, all shared within a higher state of consciousness to help assist you throughout your journey. So as you can see, it's imperative that you develop the clarity of a righteous mind, worthy of the battle, in order for your positive dreams to become reality.

Remember, we are at war within the spirit, not the flesh. So if the flesh were attacked, the spirit could suffer if not properly trained or seeded for the battle. The lack of faith would be detrimental during the battle from within. Know that which swiftly takes residence in the lack of training is often fear, and fear is one of the deadliest tools in regard to preventing forward progression.

This is why I give a certain respect to those who are stricken with various issues on this earth, those who are attacked in ways that could prevent their intended growth in power for the purpose of balance within the two realms. These people may in fact be the ones gifted to lead and bridge a much-needed gap, especially in regard to communication. Understandably, this knowledge reminds me never to judge another but rather to acknowledge their actions and have positive faith that they will once again find their way. In the acknowledgment of this principle, you could see how attacks come in various ways, seeking out a particular type of person created to be a leader but instead swayed or devoured by insecurities.

Thinking back within my journey, I've noticed three specific kinds of attacks that were closely related to visions revealed in my past. One would be the attack of the mind. This affects those who are afflicted with addiction to any form of drugs, from cigarettes to prescriptions and all illegal forms. This can also be in the form of depression, guilt, or lack of forgiveness. The demonic focus here is to keep the minds of the righteously chosen cluttered with drivel, questions, doubt, and confusion. These afflicted people could be the spirits of great leaders by example, yielding the powers of confidence while laying waste to the wiles of diabolical influences. These leaders may have possessed the ability to inspire and change the minds of the multitudes simply by walking in the presence of authority. When I encounter such a person, I have deep empathy, knowing that if they uncovered the significance of their purpose, they'd instantaneously exude lucidity within the darkness of humanity.

The second kind of attack is the attack on health; this is an indirect attack, savagely devouring self-esteem and morale by afflicting the physical temple. Earlier in the chapter, I described the playful spirits of health as one of the three kinds of spirits at the gates: within their surroundings, they heal the sick, tired, or weary; their light was a nurturing, shimmering glow. When on the battlefield, this spirit is impervious to deceptions, trickery, or unscrupulous ways set by the enemy. Its only concern is to revitalize the worthy—not to do battle but to heal and cleanse the mind, ridding it from vile and negative thoughts that in turn diminish the aura of health. On earth, these people are sought out by the demonic influences of hatred and negativity, which in turn attack with many physical diseases by way of the mind and temple.

When I encounter these stricken people, I pray that their peace be still, because within their place of solitude, they have the astounding ability to heal themselves while here on earth. The problem is that negative influences linger closely, causing feelings of depression or unworthiness within the afflicted. This manifests itself as guilt or worry, preventing the temple from being cleansed and eventually healed.

The third attack I've seen up close and personal: the attack on the voice. This is a foul attack specifically meant to devalue the truth within the soul. The first two attacks were that of mind and body, but the most significant to me is the attack on the voice that binds the body and spirit together. I regard the voice as one of the most powerful connections between the realms, because its energy transcends space and time. The gift of voice gives rise to the speaking of blessings, abundance, and confirmations for people in need. However, when the voice is attacked, it creates disbelief and feelings of unworthiness in the minds of the listeners. The demonic tools in this case would be addiction to alcohol or any other tongue-twisting substance that severs or alters the truth within the messenger. I mentioned these spirits at the gates, but didn't elaborate on the memory of the ravishing experience. As a galaxy of lights, millions upon millions gathered around as travelers to absorb and listen as the spirits the size of planets read from the palms of their hands, opening up the flowing of magnificent teachings of historical truth and stories of spiritual brilliance. As far as I could see, there were no actual books, just wisdom, truth, and knowledge, rising like the mists from enormous waterfalls reminiscent of another journey; flowing from the valley size prints of their hands.

It was shown to me: it's a mental connection to God when both hands come together in prayer, acknowledging the callouses and scars from a life's journey of sacrifice and love. An example of Christ when holding another's hand in guidance, a representation of the Holy Spirit when embracing and guiding another through harm. This was of great importance for all who travel under the cloak of dreams, but it's mind-boggling to know just how the battlefield renders most unprepared.

So often we are afraid and unaware of the power that has already been bestowed within us. Just as our hands can bring forth miracles channeled from deep within our hearts, our minds too can reach realms of destiny. Ever wonder why birds of a feather flock together, but eagles soar in complete lack of the need of an entourage? This is why the corrupt seek out others to latch on to, even though both could be free from the corruption of bondage—but only if one faithfully takes the stand and speaks freedom into existence. Remember, most are convinced we only use 10 percent of our brains' capacity; this limitation is in direct proportion to the afflictions ravaging our minds' true capabilities. In other words, instead of submitting to the strongholds of misconstrued beliefs and relying on the flock that would otherwise suffocate your hope, try believing that you're cancer free, just as confidently as you believe the sun will rise the next day. This confidence is power; it is worthy within the realm of the battle. Think about this: we breathe air because we expect to breathe air. We wouldn't try to breathe water, right? Even though we had no issue breathing water for nine months of our lives before entering this world. My point is, your body will adjust to the environment you accept into your subconscious.

A baby has no clutter between these realms, so it makes the transition and adaptation real. If the afflicted could remove the clutter, depression, guilt, or worry, their temples would make their transition back to spiritual balance.

Believe this in absolute confidence, just as you'd expect to inhale your next breath. Take it for granted if you must, that is, until confirmation seeps in. Just believe and do so before any other thoughts enter your mind. Remember, it is my prayer that you would find this power in the solitude of your peace; seek this out, and it will infinitely reveal itself. Know that many earthly afflictions speak greatly upon the spirit world. Within this realization you can have a piece of heaven on earth if you choose to pull this enlightenment into your atmosphere; this is why the true law of attraction can be so influential in a person's life if they only have faith within themselves and not the appearance of the world—hence, back to the importance of children's dreams, fairy tales, and nightmares. Fortunately, these visions had many great impacts on my personality, especially when I found myself alone, encountering the negative principalities of man made trials and tribulations.

This is how my story of valor started, as with many stories, and I speculate yours as well. We all started from knights in shining armor and princess bride beginnings, but something happened, remember? Something changed in the midst of telling our bedtime stories, something quite real, in fact—and in my case, I simply had no idea how to engage in battle, let alone understand the battle. Nevertheless, I had something to do.

Chapter 2
The Turning Point

As mentioned, in my days of youth, challenges were an everyday way of life, but I soon found out not all challenges were mine to battle, but rather to learn from. For instance I remember a turning point in my life, not so welcomed but greatly received.

A certain example comes to mind, back when I tried to engage in a battle that wasn't my own. Not so nostalgic of a memory, being it still reminds me of those lonely days. I recall one day when my parents didn't appear to get along all that well. No complaints from me, they were young and to be brutally honest it gave me more time to train for saving the world. On this day, while my mother was preparing for a Tupperware party and my father was at work, I decided to fulfill one of my desires: jumping off the top of our garage with a plastic garbage bag, thinking the wind would catch me up and parachute me back to earth gently. I was wrong. Perhaps thirty minutes passed before I woke up from my twenty-five-foot leap of faith in the backyard. Fortunately, no one was around to see my painfully excruciating failed attempt, so I brushed myself off, limped into the house, and put the garbage bag back where it belonged: in the trash. This is but a glimpse of my adventures, so to give you a better foundation of who I am, I'll share just a few more.

I'm sure most can relate, being as we've all had our nicks and bruises. This brings to mind one of the best Saturday mornings ever.

On this day, my parents were in a surprisingly playful mood, the *Bugs Bunny/Road Runner Hour* was on, and Dad was making Pillsbury cinnamon rolls—oh, how sweet was the aroma in the air. It was truly a perfect morning; my sister was nagging my big brother to no end, Mom and Dad were talking and laughing, and as for me, I was preparing to fly once again. I don't know if it was the cartoons or the smell of baked goods in the kitchen, but I somehow got the notion to play Superman. Nobody could see what I was up to, so I tied a pillowcase around my neck, stretched my arms forward, and began my flight around the house.

Up, up, and away! I recall feeling totally free within my adventure. So free that I closed my eyes momentarily. To this day, I can still feel the cool mist of the clouds brushing against my forehead—but unfortunately, my flight of triumph came to a crashing halt. I ran right through the plate-glass security door, shattering it into a shimmering cascade of brilliant crystals. My mother screamed in a way I still can't get out of my head, and neither do I care to remember the look of terror on her face. My brother's and sister's mouths were stuck wide open; their eyes were frozen in shock.

Then came the thunderous footsteps of my father charging down the hallway, ready with towels in both hands, only to see me standing on the porch, surrounded with shattered glass glimmering in the sunrise of the morning.

At this moment, I tried to utilize one of my sister's greatest assets. I dug down deep into my soul and pulled out my very saddest "please don't punish me; feed a starving child from a poverty-stricken country for only thirty cents a day" face.

No words were spoken that I can recall; I only remember the shock and confusion on my parents' faces. There was no ambulance, no falling to the knees in prayer for healing, no tears—even though I tried to bring on the waterworks. I suffered no harm, not even a scratch.

One thing I can say about that incredible Saturday is that it was the most memorable Saturday morning I had ever had. Not because of the cascading crystals yielding to my will, but because it turned out to be the last Saturday morning we'd spend together as a family ever again, being as days later would come the impending divorce. Oh, but what a day it was. I can still smell the sweet aroma of cinnamon and warm icing in the air.

I have many stories of the like that I would love to open up about, but I'll keep it to the specific ones that influenced me to write this book. As you can see, my story begins like many stories of youths growing up and taking the world by storm—but being completely honest with ourselves, we all can identify with the problematic ups and downs of life and childhood. For instance, we all know of that one child in the family who is just plain complicated; the future likelihood of success for this child would appear to be downright miserable. And I happen to be viewed as such a child.

Understandably so, I submit to you that I was very young, and life as I knew it was a bit confusing, but I also offer no excuses, because in my heart I was trying to do what I felt was right.

Retrospectively speaking, I now know I was trying to uphold my purpose, ignore my reasoning, and ultimately save my parents. I mean humorously questioning, how many kids do you know set fire to their parents' car and actually stayed in it? Yes, that was me; fortunately, my parents pulled me out in time to teach me a lesson, which was far greater than the alternative consequence of being engulfed in flames. On this day, which took place a bit before I turned six years old, altered the course of my life, this is when my perspective outlook on life started to take an interesting turn.

Understand that up until this point, I wasn't considered a problem child or worse a menace. It was more like I was considered a bit too energetic. In today's society, teachers, doctors or parental friends would have emphatically suggested getting me on Ritalin or some other mind-altering drug, which would have laid waste to my spirit-filled childhood creativity. This is but one of many reasons why I love my parents unconditionally; even though I was a handful, they still made the difficult decision not to alter my path, although I was the recipient of much discipline. Furthermore, when speaking of paths, we must acknowledge that not all roads are smooth. In fact, some paths can encounter surprisingly rough terrain. What can I say? I was the middle child, and trouble seemed to vicariously follow closely behind the footprints of my destiny.

Honestly, I was never attention seeking, yet apparently challenges were always seemingly lurking closely behind. Remember, in my reality, I was constantly preparing for battle, so the unexpected became my comfort zone as to always be prepared. This was normal behavior because I was continuously on the lookout for unexplained forces trying to hinder my path.

Some people assumed I caused issues because I wasn't getting as much attention as my siblings, but this was far from truth. In fact, I felt I was protecting them from the very forces I believed were after my soul. Despite what others may have thought, I was actually trying to avoid any competition with my big brother or younger sister.

Prior to separation, one day my parents found a babysitter up to the challenge of watching over my brother and me. I'll submit that this too was a day I'll never forget. It started like any normal day, where the parents were busy trying to balance career, life, and relationship. So, having a babysitter was an appropriate decision for such a spectacular day, being as they finally got a little time for themselves. Meanwhile, under the care of our sitter, my brother and I got permission to walk to the corner store to buy candy.

This was like striking it rich. Just the thought of candy without parental control led to a mental sugar rush! Perhaps yet and needless to say, I didn't exactly reach my intended goal. On the way back to the babysitter's apartment, we were so excited to eat our treats that we darted off running, neglecting to look while crossing the street.

I knew my brother was the fastest person on the planet; I of course was a close second, but seconds make all the difference, especially at this point in time. He made it across the street safely, but I hesitated to start at the last moment. Within a fraction of a second, I summoned the courage to follow big brother. Only something happened: a sudden dry taste paralyzed my tongue and throat, and simultaneously a sick feeling of dread clamped my chest.

It was as if the air in my lungs tugged me back a few feet. This is when my world abruptly changed, for this was the moment I got hit by a car. Later that day we found out that the driver was a nurse speeding down the road to St. Elizabeth Hospital. The story was that she was only doing about thirty-five miles per hour trying to make it to her shift. I believe she drove a light-blue 1965 Gran Torino—that is, if I heard correctly. Nonetheless, I remember tires screeching, the smell of burnt rubber over the rocky pavement, the taste of dirt and blood filling my mouth, and the sizzle of hot engine oil splattered across my face and chest. This must have all happened in a split second, but to me it was as if time slowed down, almost to a halt. In this moment, I could sense all things within the environment; all of my senses plus a few more were clear and at my discernment. As I started to explore my surroundings, time appeared to be irrelevant, based on my awareness of how slowly the debris from the pavement floated above the ground. I can remember zooming into the floating particles and visualizing them on a microscopic level, as if discovering a new planet.

I recall the taste of fresh wintergreen gum in the mouth of the driver, as well as her thought process. She was angered by her spouse, worried about her position at work, and frustrated by the sudden start of her menstrual cycle. (I don't care to ever feel that again.) This is what I have come to call a 360-degree view of my environment. It seemed to last as long as my curiosity was intrigued, but soon that sick feeling of dread came back.

The violent tug that had grasped me earlier was swiftly approaching, but this time, a sense of peace and stillness quickly came upon me, and then everything started to fade to black. The next thing I remember was getting up to my knees and stumbling to the sidewalk. Immediately I noticed a woman in the window of her house, apparently screaming at the top of her voice, only I couldn't actually hear anything.

Next, the lady ran outside and put a folded white sheet over my head. At this point, everything turned red, then to a tinted brown, and then back to black. Years later I've heard stories of people who visualized a bright light or scenes from their lives flashing before their eyes, but that wasn't my experience. The best way I can describe this near-death event is that I was being pulled swiftly in reverse, as if I were falling, but instead of going downward, I was snatched off my feet. It was as if a large hand grabbed me from the back, gripping me across my chest and torso and through my legs as if I was a rag doll, then threw me backward into a dark abyss. At this moment, everything seemed to accelerate more rapidly than I could visualize; in fact, I recall what appeared to be stars being stretched as I continued to progress faster than the speed of light.

Although I couldn't see where I was headed, I had this overwhelming sense of peace, and the further away I got, this sense of peace grew larger and larger. At this point, I could somehow feel that time, worries, and fears weren't important anymore; soon I started to be overcome with an incredible sense of breathtaking joy.

Still today I can't fully express it in words, and I doubt if it can be expressed in a way that can do it justice, but I can recall, as I was being pulled closer, all the molecules in my being began to diffuse. I then felt what could best be described as my spirit being like a grainy, clouded drop of warm water hitting the cool surface of an ocean. Instantaneously I was cleansed, made crystal clear in the purest form of ethereal energy radiating as one and all within the matter of the universe. I remember the pulsating feeling of being aware of everything, no ends, edges, or boundaries. Just a brilliant sense of peace, ever expanding in the omnipotence of pure and complete confidence. The visual sensations are hard to explain; I can feel them but can't do them justice at this point in my life.

After my brief encounter with what we describe as energy and the universe, I was pulled back toward the earth. Only this time I didn't fear the darkness, being as I understood its many purposes. What we've come to know as darkness can be misconstrued by our embedded fears.

This darkness that I encountered was a darkness of cleansing, rest, and nourishment. Why? Because my fear was completely washed away—a better description would be suctioned away—by some sort of reverse gravity.

Imagine a large, circular lake, with pure, crystal-clear water, stretching from one side of the world to the other. No bottom, just perfectly clear water, pure within itself. Now imagine how black this water gets in the center, absolutely without reflection and completely void of the sun's light as you travel deeper into the center of the earth.

After a while you would ascend to the other side of the atmosphere, but something special happens between the travel. I found rest in this darkness, no sound, movement, or clutter. There was healing in this place, a complete revitalization while traveling back to Earth. A quick but simple description of this feeling would be: imagine you're outdoors suddenly jumping out of a hot tub on a cold night. You run into the cabin and leap into a comfy bed, wrapping yourself tightly in crisp, cool sheets under a thick quilt. Tossing and turning for a moment, you shiver off the cold while tucking in your knees closely to your chest. Momentarily there's no light, no sound, just the feeling of the cold being pulled from your bones deep into the mattress, now multiply that soothing feeling of absolute bliss by a thousand.

After this brief moment of rest within the darkness, I awoke at the hospital, soon sitting straight up in the bed to find doctors surrounding me, feverishly writing every word I spoke. Only I can't remember saying anything of importance; in fact, the more I came to conscious, the cloudier my thought process became. I assume something else had a more prevalent message to speak through me, but whatever the doctors heard, they kept it amongst themselves.

Soon afterward, my father barreled his way into the emergency room, my mother was right behind him, frantically speaking all types of not-so-considerate words! The focus of concern was my forehead, being as the front temporal part of my skull was shattered into missing fragments.

I can't remember what took place as far as any conversations between my parents and the doctors, but I can recall the feeling of ease and comfort as I lay down to rest. Understand that recalling this is only possible because of the continued visions over years, released in increments from my subconscious. If I had been asked to describe this days or even weeks after that life-altering event, it would have been an impossibility, being back then I couldn't put the description of the images or feelings into words, not to mention it was impressed upon me to hold my tongue.

It was like reading the summary of a complex book: you get an idea of what it's about, but you're far from true understanding, that is, until you have committed to really absorbing the book over time and the story has seeped into your mind, revealing its knowledge, visions, and manifestations. The only issue is that the best descriptions can only be uncovered or remotely described at best by a person unknowingly entering that state of subconsciousness. So for the psychologists, neurologists, and so on, understand that this can't be humanly replicated. Even for the many who have gone through a near-death experience. Their journey could be completely different, based on what's deeply embedded in their mental storehouse. There's no drug, hypnotic procedure, or device of this world that can bring about this type of authentic experience.

The closest one could get to a vision such as this would be via some form of hallucinogen or a procedurally induced stimulatory effect to generate it in the cerebral cortex of the brain. Only this would reveal the bombardment of autosuggestions, manifested fears, and clouded perceptions of a worldview embedded since childhood.

It turns out that visions are opened and shared for distinctive purposes. Showing up ill-prepared could alter your reality and the people around you in a terrible way. If a person is chosen but does not decide to use the knowledge or in turn use it for selfish intent, the blessed knowledge may be pass to the next person, leaving void in the originally intended. The point is we can't choose; we must be chosen and upon this chosen few, must accept. Moreover the results of an induced procedure to get an idea of another realm or time in space could be vastly misinterpreted; at best.

Why? Because the visions or experiences aren't man made. If attempted replication involved human hands, ideas, or devices, the experience would not be effectively duplicated. Trust me when I say that even in the smallest forms of fundamental building blocks, such as atoms, quarks, or leptons, nothing that humans touch or manipulate as particles of matter can duplicate or bring about these experiences, even conscious thought can alter the path of an experience, rendering it to nothing more than a fallacy. This is why we seek enlightenment, being our best descriptions are limited to our understandings and imaginations of this world.

For instance, if I told you to picture the color blue, you'd immediately think of the color falling between green and violet, even though blue is a primary color. It cannot be mixed to make what "we" call blue; it's accepted that the reflection of cyan and magenta makes blue. Nevertheless, it's what we've come to see by what we were taught in the educational system. Meanwhile, blue is blue in the daytime but ask yourself, is it still blue in the darkest of night, when colors cast no reflection or absorbed light? Is any color for that matter its perceived color within the absence of illumination? My point is, since what we perceive depends on the reflection of a surface, while in the light we can only consider the nature of a thing as what we've been taught it is. So, as I said, we can only describe another realm to the best of our abilities according to the education we've been exposed to. My experience was beyond a certain amount of description because my mind has been limited by the autosuggestions that "we only have five senses" or "humans only use 10 percent of our brains' capacity." Wrong! And one of my favorites as mentioned prior "There are only twenty-six letters in our alphabet," this excludes what was historically the twenty-seventh letter, the ampersand.

This is why, as a child, when I started to hear the echoing, I took advice from another traveler and kept my mouth shut upon waking up. Know that if the curiosity of man's lust to acquire power from other realms for misguided purposes, only breeds the destruction by way of vice within the purpose, corrupting the purity of knowledge.

Again, if this is the standard of our intentions, it's no wonder why our communication within humanity is limited. It goes without saying that "out of this world experiences" are cumbersome at best, being as we lack the clarity of verbal and mental capabilities to describe them in purposeful detail.

In doing this, we tend to do our best with what we've learned. In my case, it took years for me to be able to complete enough of a mental descriptive puzzle to begin to share my experiences—that and I didn't want to be trapped by medication like my traveler friend. Humans exist because oxygen is conducive to the matter and functions that support and maintain life.

Everything we need to live, produce, and flourish as humans has been established by God, but guess what? God is so much more than human understandings; he didn't just stop at making mankind, even though our consciousness believes we're the highest forms of intelligent life in the universe. How presumptuous is that? We were giving dominion over the animals, true—but not over all that resides in the universe.

It's unfortunate that we've accepted that humans can blindly create, because truthfully, that knowledge could lead to our demise. For instance, why are we cross-engineering foods or using biomechanics to enhance or create cloned food? It was said a while ago that genetically engineered food would "feed the poor" and "stop world hunger." The only lingering issue is there are even more people starving today than twenty years ago.

Where are the miracle breakthroughs? Anything constructed with intentions, not conducive to the overall purpose of good cannot solve the problem. Why? Because the invention was created for the purposes of meeting demands, not for the purpose of doing good. Here's something to think about, a cliché I'm sure most have heard: "If it ain't broken, don't fix it!" That is until someone comes along and adds the words *new and improved*, *upgraded*, and *enhanced*, or the like so that we perceive that it *is* broken.

So, understand, insidious demands wouldn't exist without the created need, being as the nature of the need is to solidify man's false dominions. No matter how bad the "issue" is, the negative powers that be will only pacify and patch up the problem, as opposed to fixing, curing or coming up with a solution.

This is why I said about my vision, "If attempted replication involved human hands, ideas, or devices, the experience would not be duplicated." At best, we can achieve complete mental clarity, but that means reaching past enlightenment into a realm of absolute void. In this, we must lose the connection of mind, body, and soul, transitioning into the spirit as one with all, ultimately laying waste to selfishness or concealed desires.

For instance, some people are reluctant to accept the Holy Trinity, meaning that God, Christ, and the Holy Spirit exist as one but on the other hand, accept the idea that humans possess a personality within their brain equipped with an identity, ego, and superego, all the while referring to themselves as one being.

Know that if and when we succeed at becoming "as one," our thought process as we know it ceases to exist, and anything deceitful or idealistic disappears. We break the bondages of fear and time, leaving a singular purpose of nothingness in our minds. This has great purpose; the ability to reach nothingness equates to everything that is immensely good in our eternity.

So, as stated earlier, time as we have come to accept in our reality momentarily slowed down during my traumatic accident, allowing for my sudden acute awareness in cognitive ability and better yet, the weight of fear, clutter, and bondage being lifted from my consciousness. Let me elaborate with a few simple examples to provide the foundation for such a claim.

Why does holding your breath under water appear to go more quickly than holding your breath while sitting at a table or lying down? Why does time seem to speed up when you really want or enjoy something, but adversely seem to slow down dramatically when you don't care to be involved in a particular event, like going to summer school or a friend's church or being subpoenaed in court? Does time actually change, or does your mind become so focused on a particular thing that your reality in "timekeeping" changes?" When was the last time you had a good conversation? I mean, whimsically lost in the laughter of a beautiful interest, or maybe a joyful event, only to suddenly find yourself saying, "My goodness, where did the time go? Guess what: it's not time that was altered, but your perceived mental awareness. Your perception on a particular subject of interest caused you to be encompassed in such a way that time wasn't as important as your task.

Now, we've all encountered the next example at some point during our hustle-and-bustle lives, you shouldn't have a problem recalling the time when that "one car," driving just two miles under the speed limit, pulled in front of you on your way to work or business meeting, resulting in you clocking in or getting to your destination two minutes past the start of your shift!

Take some time to absorb this process—that driver doesn't even know you exist, and yet inadvertently you created a mental relationship with them that not only sped up your heart rate but also mystically appeared to slow the driver in front of you down! Why? It's because of your sudden focus and awareness—and please understand that tailgating out of a lack of patience only causes the driver to slow down even more!

My point is, time is relative to the proportion of our concentrated interests, and at the time of my incident, I was impacted by something far stronger than I could comprehend. Now, after years of piecing together the unimaginable, the truths and visions I received finally became clear. The mind has many ways of adjusting reality to fit our comforts, ideas, opinions, and perceptions. Just be careful of what you continuously focus or dwell on, for this without doubt will manifests itself into your personal beliefs. A harsh example would be that of biases or prejudices. On a much lighter side, this could also help explain why some men dread the idea of the mother-in-law visiting over the weekend.

Maybe this is why men believe Mom's cooking is the best! This is why it's important to "take the time to smell the roses."

If you're focused on the good, good things will manifest effortlessly into your reality. For instance, let's start with the average person waking up on the wrong side of the bed. Possibly it's due to celebrating a bit too much with friends the night before. Maybe it's because they are stressing over unresolved issues at work, caused by submitting their interest to that continuously gossiping coworker. Or worse yet, maybe it's from that embedded fear of not having financial security or relationship compatibility established for their loved ones.

These are just a few of the so-called realities most have come to accept and live with, but I implore you to be cautious. Changing your vision by cleansing your mind proves detrimental toward these kinds of battles from within, which in turn clears a path to your abundance by way of reaching enlightenment. Choose to slow down, breathe, and meditate for the purpose of achieving homeostasis between body and soul. On this path, confirmations will prove to be set in your journey, along with a few other gifts stored away.

Chapter 3
In the Bosom of the Holy Spirit

Going back to my childhood and revisiting the circumstances which helped developed my consciousness, may help show how I came to my enlightened ways. It began after my accident, but the truth lay dormant in the mind centuries before my vessel came to walk upon this earth. Deep within my rest, I found myself sitting on the edge of the hospital building, under a full moon, healing within the bosom of the Holy Spirit. I remember listening deep into the night while the moonlight whispered secrets on the surface waters. Like a child sharing a promise with other siblings, the moon playfully reflected all that was hidden in the cloak of night from its travels across the world.

The waters glimmered with intrigue, then ascended as a mist to share with the winds, all while speaking parables from the leaves of the trees deeply rooted in the moisture of the soil. The fulfillment of the moon created rays of violet, carried by a symphony of vibrations throughout a gentle breeze; this passed through my body like a pulse; instantaneously I was healed.

"A gift," the Holy Spirit said, but for some reason I couldn't speak. Immediately I understood that my words could not translate within this realm; if I tried to talk, it would be like talking under water. Again the spirit spoke: "Your soul is conducive within this realm to communication. Believe, and it is done."

It was at this time when I realized words weren't of the manipulation of the mouth; they were more like a feeling or a confident gesture that communicated language. Moreover, our communication was like a heartfelt feeling or a beautiful memory shared within a bond of trust. I understood, "Within this realm your voice would be similar to a bird's, chirping in the dawn of the morning."

Again, the imagery is too inconceivable to put in words, and yet my heart understood it by way of joyful tears. As long as I remained in the presence of the Holy Spirit, I was able to absorb this conveyance in the form of shared information and clear perspective. This was truly a marvelous gathering; I could feel the coolness of the flowing waters as the reflection of peace was being channeled through their light. I could hear the spirit of wisdom within a song, rhetorically rejoicing in God's silhouette upon the night's surface, especially atop the rich greenness of the trees, where it absorbed knowledge deep into its own roots. Soon afterward, I witnessed a reflection of God's light upon the moon as it opened up a glimpse of my purpose.

This interaction went on for six months, the moon revolving around the earth but never the sun. I was told by the comforter to "rest within," also that "truths are embedded in the form of seeds and with proper nourishment within the soil of your trials, purposes will be birthed into existence. Some truths are to be spoken, some are to be written but most will be passed on to my children and whom I lead by example."

This is but a fragment of the analogy that was impressed upon my spirit. By itself the moon is dark within the coldness of the universe, but when graced with the reflection of the sun's light, it instantaneously creates balance, purpose, and wisdom within the earth. In other words, when we are spoken to, we use our ears to channel the vibrations from another's voice, their voice that derives from the spirit of intentions within their consciousness.

We then use sight to articulate and coordinate body language with this sound to interpret and understand. However, our understanding and perceptions of words are constantly under attack by our own weighted consciousness; we filter words into meanings that best reinforce our embedded ideas, concerns, or fears. This is why the heart continuously reaches for balance and companionship, while the battle between the heart and mind creates an imbalance within the channels of enlightenment. Even though your heart feels the beauty within the truth, the embedded thought process of the mind quickly clouds its nature by trying to make sense of the blessed essence of love, peace, and happiness.

In other words, fruit was meant to be eaten. Let the nourishment take hold and maintain the essence of life within your body—don't dissect the fruit to figure how or why it is; just eat and fulfill the covenant. If the heart and mind become locked in struggle, the victor may produce a void that disconnects body and soul. This is where selfishness breeds a sense of abandonment, then leads to a spirit of challenge and measurement of self-worth through pride and hierarchy.

This, as mentioned before, leads to false dominion upon the earth and inadvertently, false mastery of the mind. Though the heart is of the sun, the mind is of the moon; the heart yields its higher power deeply within the subconscious mind in perfect balance, and this sacrifice protects the body of earth and its purpose within the true meaning of life. Within this sacrifice, the warmth of the heart still resonates through the darkness, and know that the darkness of the mind serves for great purpose. Furthermore, remember the gravity of the earth manifests its balance upon the land, wind, and waters. No different from the gravity of your spirit and how it relates to your temple, the blood in your veins and the air you breathe.

Therefore, the mind's reflection upon the heart, through the darkness of the flesh, must be in balance to hold the gravity of its spirit. The channels cannot be broken, lest there be unbalance within the temple, in which case the human purpose would be halted. Ever wondered what would happen if the Earth stopped spinning on its axis due to the moon's gravitational pull? Well, that's like the power of the heart within you. Ask yourself: What is your heart pulling you to do? I can assure you it's doing what it was created to do since the beginning of time, seeking to reconnect within the nature of your love, peace, and abundance.

Seek this path of truth and you'll diminish any life-draining fears or embedded traps within your consciousness. It's imperative to acknowledge any weakness that would otherwise sabotage your purpose. For instance, if I asked you the question, "Is your mind a reflection of God's light in the darkness of your flesh?"

Would you take it to heart seriously, or would an embedded vision of a supernatural being—or lack thereof—immediately block the purpose of the enlightened question, revealing the weakness of guilt? What is sight if it's clouded by the embedded misconceptions of the mind? Understand that a journey without a path leads nowhere. You can live without your eyes, but try living without knowing your purpose. I ask you to change your position; you don't need to receive a vision to receive the light in question. It doesn't matter who you think God is—most don't even know who *they* are, even when standing in front of a mirror—but the laws of the universe are and will always be, forevermore. This brings to mind a dream I had when I was thirteen years old; it was between the Trinity of this world and a man fishing.

One day a man went fishing for his family. Confident within himself, he cast out his net into the waters and waited for fish to take the bait. After hours had passed without a catch, a feeling of frustration came over him. The thought of his family, hungry, increased his dread, but deep within his heart he felt heavy. By the pull of this feeling, he fell to his knees in the sand and placed his hands in the water, submitting aloud, "Please! Please produce fish for my family!" Suddenly, many fish appeared, and he rejoiced in the waters and gave praise, saying, "Water, I owe you my life!" Upon this, the presence of the water spoke: "I am of the water, not of its name." Shocked, the man gazed upon the infinity of the waters and replied, "But you've given me a great bounty of fish; you must be the greatest power of all.

Again the voice within the water spoke: "You are of my seed and therefore the power within you was manifested upon the submission of your heart. This brought forth the bounty of your will." The fisherman asked, "Who are you? What do I call you?" He was answered, "I am the land in which you sow, the air in which you breathe, and the water in which you consume. I am all within the Trinity as one. Names are of this world, bestowed only to the uniqueness of man. No other being goes by name.

A tree as you've named it will produce as it does regardless of any name given; it is what its purpose proves to be, which is the reason for its creation. "If you'd encounter another who called the tree differently or came to know it by a different understanding, it would be of no difference to the nature of the tree. It would still bear its fruit, provide shade, and submit nourishment to man."

The fisherman then asked, "To whom do I lay down my body in honor of my life?" He was answered, "Do your children owe you their lives, killing themselves in the name of your love? Death is swift, like a fallen seed from the sunflower plant hitting the ground, but the life span of the embedded seed begins within the soil and reveals a much greater cycle to fulfill; it is in this journey the seed endures the rigors of life, breaking through the crust to one day open up within the light of my glory.

Go and nurture your children, wife, and brethren unconditionally as I've nurtured you.

You are favored to exist—the elements of the earth are conducive to you, and within the elements you exist by way of my presence. Submit to this truth, for this covenant is the purpose of life."

Within my understanding, this dream gives me the freedom to love and worship without the onslaught of opinions and impressions suggested by tainted others. I am, because he is, and he resides in me as well as you; this makes us "as one" within God and his purposes for life. This explains why we possess the power of life or death within our words, no different from the man submitting for the bounty of fish. If you believe it shall come to pass, your thoughts as well will manifest in you and then come to pass as well.

Be careful of the beliefs you hold in your heart, for the presence of God resides in you, knowing this is just the beginning of your righteous journey. Once I worked with a friend who claimed to be an atheist. He said, "I don't believe in a God that would let children die and suffer across the world." I replied, "That's fine. We all have our opinions, but do you believe in your physical being? Are you real? If so, who created your body or the life-force you call your own?"

He smiled and answered my question with a statement, followed by his own question. He said, "There's no answer to that. That's like the old question: What came first, the chicken or the egg?" I smiled and said I figured that one out back in the first grade. I answered that the creator of the egg was first.

He replied, "Well, I guess I don't believe in a God at all," so I said, "That's fine; we all have our respective opinions, depending on what pace we're at in life, but why did you blame a God for letting children die and suffer across the world?" He cleverly replied that that was just a saying, but added, "I do believe in a higher, supernatural being, though."

I said, "Wow, me too! Does this supernatural being prevent children from dying and suffering across the world?" He emphatically said, "No that's God's doing," with a smile on his face. "It's all just a game, but I'm a good person. I just don't like someone giving me rules for how to live my own life."

I then said, "I understand where you're coming from. I don't particularly like working under our boss, but we have a job that more than pays the bills. So, I'm thinking you're actually rebelling against people shoveling all the hellfire and brimstone stories down your throat, right?"

He emphatically replied, "Yeah, That's crazy! My grandma and high school teacher were the same way, not to mention my parents made me go to church like three days a week, and they fought more than anyone I know. I'm not perfect, but I deserve to make it into heaven just like anyone else!" I told him, "I believe without a doubt that you will make it into heaven." He looked dumbfounded and said, "How's that possible if I'm not a slave to all his rules and regulations?" Swiftly I said, "I don't consider them to be regulations at all but rather, absolute laws create for our peace on earth.

Laws that solidify and uphold the balance of life as we know it." But I could tell this was a little over his head. So I said, "In your case, consider yourself already in, per Calvary. First, simply believe God exists, and this belief will strengthen you to one day overcome all doubt, guilt, pain, or confusion that comes from the negative persuasions that plague your mind.

In accepting this, it'll provide you with an impenetrable foundation to rest, stand, or lean upon in a time of need. "Furthermore," I asked, "Do you really believe you'd be a slave, or do you have a choice within the free will of your spirit?" He didn't reply, but confusion was on his face, and then he uttered, "Well, I've never felt free!" I said, "That's probably because of all the programmed misinformation by way of the negative heterosuggestions you've fallen victim to in your life."

Just when I thought a person's forehead couldn't wrinkle any further, he said, "What are you talking about? I control what goes on in my head; no one knows what I think or feel." I replied, "It's not your words that make you who you are but, rather, your actions." I said, "Ever wonder why a TV show is called a television *program*? It tells your vision what's to be programmed deeply within your mind. How about a sitcom? This actually tells your mind to 'sit calm' and be amused! So what of primetime television? You guessed it—this is the projected time the media deems worthy, with the greatest number of people to be influenced, programmed, or persuaded; hence the millions of dollars spent on advertising by way of commercials during these specific times or times like the Olympics or the Super Bowl.

Most people lead their lives by the winds of persuasion without even knowing it. "Ever walked into a store to buy one thing, and you leave with ten other items that are not remotely necessary, but suddenly you craved and bought them anyway? How about driving home after work knowing there's food there for dinner, but you get fast food anyway? We've become so desensitized to persuasion tactics that we pay them no attention.

"Last example," I said to my friend. "Why are you wearing those expensive basketball shoes?" He said, "Because I like the ballplayer who wears them. I sacrificed for these babies—they just came out!" I said, "Nice. What did he buy of yours? Does he even know you exist?" He said no, and I said, "Not true! Even though the ballplayer has never seen you, he's very aware of your existence because of the sacrifice you made to buy his product. In fact, the ballplayer's faith in your contributions strengthens his actions on the court—he believes in you, so he works hard to keep your interest." He then replied, "You're full of sh**!"

I said, "That's fine; we all have our opinions—but answer me this: who persuaded you to buy the shoes? Or better yet, what came first, the ballplayer or the game?" He said, "Whoever created the sport." I smiled and said, "Very clever, Then you do believe in a creator worthy of your sacrifice." Know that either way you perceive it, the acknowledgment of God is a start in the right direction. Is it so troublesome to fill your heart with the goodness of his covenant?

Here's the takeaway, don't take the easy way out and allow anyone to create distractions or loopholes within the absolute laws of his provisions to sway you away from being the person you were born to become. Please, do not allow a false prophet to cause you to detour toward a rebellious nature, because that would mean you submitted your trust into the idol and not the unfathomable wisdom of the truth, dwelling within the enlightenment of your spirit."

If that's too much to suddenly hold, just know that it's better to have faith and not need it than to need it and not have faith. We've all fallen short of the glory of God, and with his mercy at least we're given a chance. Besides, not all who come back from life-or-death experiences bring something special back. It depends upon your battlefield preparations here on earth; that dictate how much knowledge you can bring back, if any. So I implore you: don't wait until an incident comes around to "see the light." Also, if you're like me—and I believe many of you are—simply hold on tight. I've had exactly seven life-or-death experiences in my life, and believe me, they don't get any easier.

REGINALD O'NEAL GIBSON

Chapter 4
Against the Grain

The friend I mentioned in the previous chapter is not alone; most people's feelings concerning difficult topics are touchy at best. I believe a lot of people are simply confused, and rightfully so, especially when you think of the large amount of misleading content out there, spewing its deceptions upon the world. Mentally, gut feelings are being compromised; physically, morals are being attacked; and spiritually, foundations are being uprooted by negative influences.

It's no wonder people get frustrated so easily or draw in defensively when they're challenged or questioned about their beliefs. I had a mentor once who boasted occasionally, "I don't discuss religion, politics, or relationships with people, especially coworkers!" I thought, *Wow! Those are very important topics, and personally I'd want to discuss them to see if I stand to be corrected.* I knew that way I'd develop a foundation of right or wrong to protect my opinion from being influenced by political ads, reality television shows, or relationship haters! Since I was looking up to this gentleman as a mentor, I could see the proverbial ceiling that would hold back my spiritual progression.

Besides, how can you trust a person that holds onto his opinion so tightly that his mind doesn't have the opportunity to develop and grow?

I asked him why the restriction, and he said, "That way you don't offend the people you're trying to create a bond with." I responded, "So, what if you encounter a person who believes something completely opposite of what you believe?"

He said, "Look at it this way: I'm going to agree with whatever makes me happy or gives me a check to cash!" Needless to say, this man was no longer a mentor in my life. He had the position, but he didn't possess the character needed to break through the ceiling of his own created barriers. Following him would have led me to a dead end in my personal development, since he submitted his position to the will of others. How could I follow such a shallow person? A true leader by definition will stand for something, as opposed to falling for nothing of true purpose; I say this as acknowledgment, not judgment. He would have no doubt continued to siphon my energy, build his legacy off the back of my hard work and naive generosity.

I've come to the conclusion that some people may not have a valid foundation in which to make a stand on at all, especially when it comes to important topics. I'm thinking it's because of lack of commitment to an overall cause. In other words, it's easier to agree, become opinionated, be persuaded on a particular topic, or just remain undecided. The only issue with passive ways is that they leave room for you to be manipulated or led astray from otherwise discovering the truths of the matter for yourself. I apologize if "lack of commitment" is too harsh, but I know that commitment is critical for awakening the thought process. Also, if more and more people become followers, then a shift in power takes place, causing an imbalance.

Imagine waking up one morning and finding that everyone in your state voted to have your home quarantined for fear of you burning it down because you don't know how to cook properly. What would you do? Who would intercede on your behalf once everyone started to follow the misguided opinions of others? Worse yet, for the "powers that be," what's their idea for your future—or is their motivation strictly for their own purposes, family traditions, or beliefs?

This understanding applies to all heads of households or people in authoritative positions, including your boss, spouse, business partners, and even friends. My mentor stood for absolutely nothing, being as he relinquished his true potential for a check. Ask yourself who's leading you and for what purpose? If there's any indication that you'll lose your way in the overall sacrifice of being a follower, you may want to rethink your path. I'm not suggesting that being a follower is a bad thing, but rather that you must faithfully have your destination in mind while being led—that way you'll at least know where to get off.

Know that we're all on a path, but ask yourself if your path is being influenced by greed, money, or power. A better question, is your path being pushed by insecurity, desperation, or fear? Even worse, is your path not your own, but rather one belonging to someone or something who will as mentioned earlier, siphon your energy to fuel their progress? These questions are meant to make you look deeper into your worth.

If you feel you're lacking in self-worth, trust me you're not! Someone or some business has noticed your potential and is probably trying to find a way to tap in if they're not already sucking the energy out of you—energy like physical strength, motivation, leadership, or even happiness. Yes, all is valuable! Depending on the purposes of the one trying to control, you may be used for your image, your body, even your happy disposition. For instance, a quick example is how a reality show seeks people that look, act or speak a certain way as to bring in the most viewers. I understand this concept in its entirety, being I was on many occasions used, taken advantage of and fallen into both categories as being codependent and that of an enabler, a good majority of my life. Point is, even on your worst days of low self esteem and misguided morals, you have great value; be careful not to allow someone to sneak in and take advantage of your true worth.

It doesn't make a difference if a person feels worthless or not, someone can pick up on the potential and figure out what works for them. Take your classic job interview: you are immediately being assessed on how much revenue you can bring into the company. Of course you get a little in return, but remember to keep your destination in mind, lest you end up a stepping stone for another person's dreams.

Look at it this way; here's a classic power shift most people often choose to ignore or simply sweep under the proverbial rug. I call it the downhill-shift. In a television commercial, a teenage girl views a flawless-looking model who is surrounded by friends while on a mall shopping spree.

I'll keep it short, but what impression is this giving the girl at home? I know it's widely accepted in our society, but there's a power shift that happens when the girl judges her own skin, smile, or body, thinking that's what she is supposed to look like. So to compensate, she figures the next best thing to do is to buy the product the advertisement is selling.

In this, the girl's money is spent empowering sales at the expense of her self-image and peace of mind. If this doesn't seem to relate to the title of this book, let me illustrate it like this: the creation of an idol leads the consciousness to false worship. Please understand the woman is the most powerful being we have walking this planet, and if something were to wreak havoc in her mind at an early age, then future generations would suffer from her conflicted self-esteem. Think about this: the female has been given the power of creation in the womb; life would not exist without her.

Okay, for all the analytical, I get it—she needs male sperm to spark the process. But let's face it—our few seconds of bliss pales in comparison to nine months in the womb. I mean, let's get off our high horses for a minute, guys, and humble ourselves; as omnipotent as God is, he created woman second for a reason! He could have started with her complete, without the need of our contribution, but thanks to his divine purpose and design, here we are. I'm really, really glad he thought it worth his time to create man, even though we've shown to have many faults.

I could go deeper, but I'll refrain from going down that rabbit hole until my next book.

Just remember, finding out who you are by trusting in yourself requires faith and commitment to a higher purpose. If you can quiet the chatter within your mind, you can hear the purpose within your heart. So, how do you "quiet the chatter"? Find a dark, quiet place, breathe deeply a few times, and focus on peace, focus on healing.

Ignore any negative thoughts, sensationalistic ideas, memories, or lust; submit your will by not trying to figure everything out per the insecurities of the embedded mind and just rest. No alarm clock, cell phone notifications, or wake-up call, just peace and health; consider this a start.

After getting into the paradigm of quieting the chatter, buckle in, because you'll start noticing the stumbling blocks placed upon your path. For instance, you'll deal with the corruptions of what you may have accepted in your life prior to going against the grain. For example, adultery, alcoholism, gluttony of any kind, hatred or lust just to name a few. You'll notice mental and physical sensitivities rise within your temple; old friends will start becoming irritating, commercials and ads will feel more condescending and insulting. Quite possibly that job or relationship you settled for will begin to rub you the wrong way.

Please do not let these minor frustrations detour you. Believe in your process and accept these agitations, because their antagonistic nature will be the push you'll need to get over the remaining obstacles in your head. After dealing with your consciousness a bit, you'll deal with the people you've placed in your environment.

Here is where you'll start to gain the momentum needed to break through the next level of embedded perceptions—your own opinions. Yes, quickly back to you and the way your thought process works. See, you'll deal with your consciousness, then your environment, and then your mind-set again. By doing this, you'll bring back the clarity of a guilt-free nature by way of forgiving others for blocking your path and letting go of deceptions otherwise hindering your decision-making abilities as well as truth. You'll finally find the humility of being able to submit to a higher consciousness, when this is done you'll find that dark, quiet place in which to breathe.

Now you're getting stronger—your field of energy is growing immensely—but know others of concealed ill intent can also pick up on your newfound positive energy—get ready to deal with them next, and remember that the key word here is *acknowledgment*. When the opportunity presents itself, as the insidious blind start to spew their nonsense, acknowledge it and be prepared to counter by standing firm in your God-given purpose to live and love by Christ's example. Some may have been scorned by self-proclaimed prophets or one of those "holier than thou" types and felt let down when they witnessed that person not living by what they preached. For instance, have you ever been sexually hit on or verbally assaulted by someone who persistently told you, "I'm spiritual or religious," or—my favorite—"I'm a Christian," all to gain your trust, confidence, or conversation? It's unfortunate that people use whatever means necessary to gain trust, take advantage of, or manipulate others, but recall I spoke about this prior.

It's simply the state of the principalities of this world. Abuse of authority behind a badge, position, or rank is all a part of the agitating principles that keep us aware of the demonic influences that roam the earth.

Some people are so far distracted in their misguided purposes, they become easily influenced by even the simplest of suggestions, including those lurking closely within our environment. Here's a quick example: You're driving to the amusement park with your family, it's a beautiful day, and everyone is happy—that is, until someone speeds past you and gives you the finger! Most people will react in a negative fashion, taking on the frustration or misguided anger of the ignorant person who gave the gesture. If your mind isn't guarded well, you may return the gesture, speed up to the car honking your horn, give them a cold stare, or even curse aloud. Why do this? Please reframe your mindset away from this spiritual entrapment!

Understand that the person's issue, gesture, or opinion of your driving shouldn't dictate your feelings or your purpose in regard to enjoying the day with your family. But if you take offense, you may inadvertently allow the ignorant suggestion to completely alter the course not only of your destination, but also of your family's day. Ever wonder how many road-rage accidents or deaths occur each year? It's hard to measure, being as the official police report would probably read, "A driver lost control of his car on I-75 today, causing a deadly chain reaction," and it's not like the driver who originally gave the gesture would stick around to tell the actual truth of the matter. It would just be another sensationalistic special report at 6:00 p.m.

Too dramatic? I don't think so. In my early twenties, I was going through a very insecure time in my life. I was struggling within "the struggle" to keep my family safe, being as we lived close to a dangerously violent drug-infested neighborhood. One night we heard shots ring out just blocks away, so I decided to take the family out and enjoy the colorful light show near the downtown riverscape. Afterward, my family and I felt great; it was truly a beautiful night as we headed back to our car, the absence of violence was a welcome blessing—until this guy pulled up to a screeching stop across the street.

I could tell he had two teenagers in his car, but I didn't understand what caused his next actions. I looked over at him in concern, and that was when he started yelling out profanity and racial slurs! Immediately I rushed my family into the car, grabbed my gun from under the seat, and fired a warning shot in the air.

Really dumb, right? Well, my clouded perception of the world led me to believe my actions were justified; furthermore, I thought I was warning them not to advance in our direction. I was wrong. Instead of driving off, he sped right toward us! So I sped off, trying to lose them in what was a barely drivable car to begin with. Minutes later and still speeding, I drove into the darkest area of the feared, drug-infested neighborhood I mentioned prior, and yes, the other car was right behind me! This had officially become a dumb-and-dumber type of situation. I stopped and jumped out my car; my family was confused and frightened out of their minds, not only by the event that was taking place but also by our current location.

So, there I was, looking absolutely ridiculous, standing beside my car, gun in hand, while the other car pulled up and just sat there with its headlights turned off. Moments later, frozen in the fear of a standoff, another guy seemingly came out of the shadows and approached me, not at all intimidated by the gun I was holding. He said, "What's up with that car tailgating you like that?" I said, "I don't know. I think he doesn't know what a 9mm is!" So the guy started to walk over to the other car, and that's when they backed up and pulled away.

Still today, I don't know who made the dumbest move that night, but I do know that if I had ignored the racial slur, I would not have put my family in danger to begin with, not to mention I would have taught my children something very different. Here's what I want you to know: First, never give a hateful gesture or express yourself in a negative way out of misguided perceptions, even if angered. You never know how deeply corrupted, demonically influenced or violent another person can be, not to forget what issues they're currently going through in life.

Second, notice that even though I so-called "tried to take my family away from the violence," I found the violence embedded within me, and it led us to the origin of what we were trying to escape. This is why I said earlier, that some people are so far gone or distracted by their clouded thinking that they become easily influenced by even the simplest of suggestions—including their environment. In this case, the violence from a nearby area suggested that I should get a gun to fight fire with fire so to speak, even though I know that to truly fight a fire, all you need is water!

The bottom line is we were both horribly wrong. If you look closer, you'll see that prejudice and ego led that guy and his family into a very dangerous situation, and my own ignorant perceptions and foolish pride did the same.

Neither one of us was better than the other, being as at that moment we fell victim to our own deeply rooted fears, a win-win for the demonic forces at work. This was over twenty-three years ago, so don't take offense at my transparency; just know that we've all been through terrible things, and we've all grown. Thinking back on the previous incident, I acted no different, mentally, than the friend I was trying to get to admit he believed in God.

In his case, he continuously justified his rebellious nature, being he felt he was constantly targeted by people trying to scare him into the submission of the believer. As it relates to the car chase incident, my friends reasoning, pointing fingers of shame probably created the negative suggestions about God, leading to his interpretation. I did the same thing, believing that since someone yelled a racial slur at me, all the racist violence in the history of the world was about to unleash an all-out assault on my family. In short, my friend and I fell victim to the spirit of fear. Even though in the car chase debacle, that guy's opinion was his own, and I can't let the negative opinions of others change the course of my path—and neither should you. Remember, the demonic forces don't care about race, gender, or creed; their only care is causing misguided perceptions.

Just be aware: these forces are patiently plotting a scheme of entanglement, but only using your own temptations, insecurity, or submissions. Yes, even though the demonic forces are real, they can't physically harm or touch you! They are as real as the negative people who cling to your interests and everyday personal businesses, devouring your blessed ideas, cleverly adding unnecessary questions meant to distract you, and tempting you with their perceptions of reality.

Whether they are your acquaintances or not, it may be their influence is of a far more sinister being; that's a risk you take when you engage with others not willing to chance the journey. Be truthful with yourself as I did when the day comes for you to evaluate your surroundings. Question yourself: are the people around you a reflection of who you are currently, who you used to be, or who you intend to be in the future? Remember, negative influences can be quick witted and subtle when they speak corrupted ideas and suggestions according to our own personal fears or shortcomings. After all, they've been close for years, taking note of all our failed attempts, mistakes, and embarrassments.

If I had a nickel for every time that one person (who never really cared for me) asked, "Hey, Reggie, you still in school? Did you pass that difficult class? Are you still going to be a chef?"

Really think about it—maybe they're closer than you're willing to accept at this moment in life; that's okay.

Just know that change will happen. When or if you want to rise above it, you'll have to change as well or simply play the part of bending to another's will.

As for me, I went through a time of denial, so I migrated toward people who pretended to share my insecurities, lust, addictions, or perceived goals. Either way, most have come to a point in their lives when it is an absolute must to take account of our growth. Whether it be knowledge, health or wealth, all in need shall come to pass but first accept that none of the acquisitions of spiritual awareness are worthwhile, without the addition of wisdom.

REGINALD O'NEAL GIBSON

Chapter 5
Let's Talk About It

Here's a thought, consider the topic of growth in any relationship. If you've been close to someone for years and there's no growth, advancement, or forward motion, whether in career, health, spirit, or finances, something's not adding up. Understand that one plus one equals two in all that we've come to acknowledge as humans. This means that two singular items became "as one," to produce an addition or forward movement that would complete the process of a third item being confirmed correct, forward in process or complete.

For instance, a man and a woman come together to produce child, diet plus exercise leads to weight loss, and watering a plant helps it flourish. When two forms of energy collide as one, something special evolves. If it's not special, consider that something may be a miss, decaying, leading to certain death and the only thing that evolves from a dead relationship is an abomination of the true purpose in life. Try watering a plant that has died and hardened within the crust, or maybe go on a diet without eating healthy, fresh, live food. Lastly, try having an interaction with a person who really isn't there; the results are indicative of a dead relationship, something to avoid at all costs! Everything we think, verbalize, and put into action equates to something, returning the effort we put in.

We invest to get a return, whether it's money invested for the interest, love for a healthy family and relationship, or prayer for salvation; we all have a fundamental desire for advancement of some sort in our lives. Recall hearing the saying "You'll reap what you sow," or as some today like to call it, the law of attraction. What I'm saying is, we've all been stuck at some point in our lives. So why put effort into something that has proven not to produce positive returns?

This isn't to say you should give up on people in need, but don't submit to a person who's taking all you have, intentionally or not; this only proves negative for both sides. If this occurs, the mental and physical strength it takes for you to journey along the path will be siphoned by the very forces I spoke about earlier. Remember, it doesn't matter what we call them, demonic forces or negative people; they will produce as they do regardless of any name given, for they are what their purpose proves to be, like the tree example the voice on the sea gave the fisherman. So whether you accept it now or later, your righteous path and purpose already exist. Moreover, when the crossroads of will and destiny abruptly presents itself, don't stress—you will choose the righteous path.

While on the topic, let me reintegrate more specifically with a quick "earthly" test revealing the devourers or dead relationships around or within your life. Whether it's a coworker, old friend, new acquaintance, mentor or even spouse, just acknowledge them and refrain from labeling. As of the day you met this person, have your bank accounts, pursuit of education, inspired ideas, health, or level of peace decreased?

This by no means suggests that a sudden increase in materialistic goods means a new or better relationship, but be honest with yourself: is your circle in forward motion, or is it laying flat on its side, draining your energy like a hole in the ground?

Does it come with strings, complications, or shrouds of confusions? If so, be careful, because first trust is established, then comes the seeping of your purpose, life advancements, or blessings, suddenly your purposes are on the back-burner weighing heavily on your conscious. Now, back to my original point regarding hidden devourers. Subtle implications from devious doers can cleverly set in place what I call "the corrupted trinity process." This is what you accept or passively allow mentally, spiritually, or physically by allowing someone else to whisper, "If I were you, I'd…" This is why I hold no regard for people whispering to me, whether it's their opinions or information.

Unbeknownst to them, for me, whispering ranks up there with gossiping, rumors, and lies. My childhood produced this dislike for whispering, for a liar, con artist or pedophile was always whispering, "It's our little secret," or "Don't tell anyone because you'll get into big trouble."

This is why I've taught my children not to keep secrets from their mother or I, even if it's for a surprise. And while on this controversial topic, I do not teach my children to believe in the whole Santa Claus thing or in the Peter Cottontail's Easter propaganda.

Why? Because I don't want them to come home from school one day, disappointed, saying, "Daddy lied to us!"

Telling these stories makes a person no cleverer than the devious doers I spoke of earlier, being as in my case I would have just been demeaning the intelligence of my children (and children are the second most powerful beings walking this planet). Honestly, how would I gain their trust in my teachings or in the great teachers of the world, if I bring them up thinking, "true leaders of humanity lie?"

How can I teach my children the followings of Christ and any other great spiritual influencers, teachers, or philosophers if I corrupt their trust? Some people argue, "Those stories never affected me," yet their connections with life and their children are most often in complete turmoil. In the many cases like this, I simply smile and say, "That's okay. We all have our opinions." Let's break the process down a bit, starting again with the bombardment of your mental storehouse. The forces of evil can wreak havoc in your life if you think, focus, or meditate on anger, including jealousy, envy, or hate. These emotions not only welcome manifestations of sickness, depression, and stress in your body but give rise to them in your actions as well, further draining the clarity of your mind. When speaking about demonic forces and other spiritualities, above all you must remember not to make false gods out of coveted creatures or images. This is a perfect example of possession by spirits. Most would say, "Not me! I'm not possessed!" But let's look a bit deeper.

When you establish a covenant, it's an agreement or contract, and when you create or establish an idol, you've just submitted to worshiping this image as a god. This is where the wiles of demonic influences creep into the mind.

Remember, this is upon your own submission! Again, most people would say, "No, not me! I've seen *The Exorcist*, and I'm not letting any spirits take over my mind, body, or soul!" Understandably so—who in their right mind would want to be possessed by other beings? But let me ask you this: Have you ever wondered why when most people get in an argument, they feel at that point that they are the smartest person in the world?

This is because they meditated on the circumstances in anger, sometimes for an hour or so before they even interacted with the other person in question! They focused on and visualized the premeditated, heated debate, exaggerated points, low blows, and punch lines. Truth is, anger has now summoned a negative spirit to convince the arguer or influence the argument in a selfish attempt to degrade the opposition. Okay, some may not be ready to agree with my understanding about the mental preparation for arguments, but know that negative forces are so devious that, once they're accepted into your mind, they continue to siphon your power by helping you recall a problematic situation that took place even years prior, causing you to daydream about coming out on top of that old laid to waste argument that has already been settled, put to rest, and in most cases completely forgotten about by the other person. This is why being scornful is a spiritual trap; remember, nothing will ever grow or be produced from the scorched earth.

Having said this, please catch yourself if you wake up on the wrong side of the bed saying, "If anyone says anything to me crazy today, I'm going to lose it!" Be careful; don't speak into existence thoughts that may not be your own!

Remember that the power of life or death resides in your vocabulary. I'll give you a better example of the manifestation of verbal and mental powers you bring into physical reality on a day-to-day basis, most without you even realizing it. Also understand any form of created image or idol you willingly accept into your mind for the purpose of drawing from its idealistic strength can summon its true being into your temple! Want a better example? Why do people get tattoos of lions, dragons, tigers, or skulls on their bodies? Why, before an athletic event or challenge, do some people take on the images of wild beasts on their jerseys or the imagery of powerful animals in their minds?

Know that submitting your temple for the purpose of summoning creatures or entities, especially ones that were originally given to us to have dominion over, could cause a shift in the spiritual balance of your life. Ever heard of using charms, orgonite, crystals, or any other objects of belief for the purpose of drawing in energy? This is yet another example of how powerful the mind is! However, using objects to focus or harness power can backfire, as these are simply idols of worship. For instance, if a person uses a charm to ward off evil, then he or she places faith in the man made object. This in turn takes away from the power of faith God gave us within the Holy Spirit. Christ died and rose again for us to utilize this power to intervene on our behalf in times of need.

If we put this power of faith into things not meant to bring fruit, we get an abomination instead! Superstition is a lie, manifested into reality by our own mental powers! This is why Jesus said the power of life or death is in the tongue.

Beware holding on to an object like a lucky rabbit's foot, as you could inadvertently bring something other than luck into your life. Ask yourself this: What weighs more, a dollar bill or a one-hundred-dollar bill? Some would beg to differ, believe it or not, but the difference in value is only based on what our minds deem worthy as illustrated on the print. If you were to close your eyes and have a friend place the dollar in one hand and the hundred in the other, you couldn't tell the difference. This is why it's said that "the love of money is the root of all evil." In other words putting your faith, trust and consciousness on the value of perceived worth, leads to false perceptions. Only in this case something develops and unfortunately its often greed or lust.

Now recall, even though the weight of the paper is the same, the mind empowers the representation of the typography. Whether it's a tattoo, a printed shirt, or even a book—what power is your mind drawing from the ink? Will it be strength, power, or knowledge? Either way, usher in what's beneficial for your destiny rather the wiles of temptation. Be careful when submitting your will to something suggested to be more powerful than the creation of your life. Being as we're in a perpetual state of spiritual war within the mind, you may want to consider what's taking root in the field of your mental battles. The phrase I used earlier was *forces are patiently plotting a scheme of entanglement*—but only by the submission of your free will.

This includes lusts, temptations, or insecurities. Again, without the submission of your free will, negative influences, demonic forces, self-doubt, as well as guilt can't harm you. Only the acceptance into your mind fully manifesting the power of fear can bring sickness into your temple. This brings up the last example of the corrupted trinity process. As just mentioned above, consider saying this over and over again as an affirmation within your thought process, as well as speaking it aloud. "the forces of evil can not physically harm me.

Now when it comes to the acceptance of physical agents like drugs, alcohol, and careless actions like anger, those are the exceptions to the rule. Just like submitting to depression or negative perceptions, falling for the after-effects of these issues can harm you internally. In addition, if you're tempted to drink, get drunk, and drive, you've allowed a mind-altering substance within your temple, and this situation could bring about the abrupt end of your physical life. Ever wonder why alcohol is often referred to as *spirits*? That's because it influences the nonphysical part of the body, often bringing out its true characteristics of insecurities.

When it comes to the indulgence of lust, it makes no difference if it's sex, drugs, or excessive shopping. The lust for anything not conducive to your purpose—even money—can destroy the temple you've been given. Know that all people were created to be wealthy, but somewhere within the fabric of time, the lust for money, power, and control manifested itself into the unbalanced of our conscious state of mind.

When you accept the lack of mental clarity caused by lust, it tends to replace the faith and trust needed to maintain a strong fellowship with your consciousness. Now instead of focus you have fear, instead of assurance you'd dwell in doubt and in place of abundance, you've birth indigence. This need not be, this is not your destiny.

Here's another quick example of how the power of the mind influences or call into reality a certain spirit. Again hold out your hands with your eyes closed and instead of money, touch, hold or even shake the hands of unknown people of different ethnic background. Can you tell which hand is of a different race?

It isn't until you open your eyes until your thought process is flooded with the embedded imageries or influences by your upbringing before you experience the manifestation of either a positive spirit such as compassion or the opposite such as racism; where's your conscious now. Also know that attacks are often indirect, again a win-win for the patiently waiting forces of entrapment. The devil can't kill you! Why? Because for starters he didn't create you, and he is not a part of this realm. The best he can do is tempt or influence your mind, which is why it's vitally important to guard your thoughts until enlightenment. People should stop giving the devil credit for their own personal mishaps, blunders, and self-induced barriers.

Fortunately, Christ sacrificed and rose again so we could live an abundant life on earth and find eternal happiness in heaven.

A few more things to remember: First, the soul and spirit are different entities, but they can be interchangeable in text, depending upon the subject matter being written about.

Second, be careful what you consume or accept into your mind, being as it can divert your true purpose and cause a change of course in your spirit. Understand that evil intent wants to convince you without the backing of the truth, so a person's weak or slow development in character could after a while cause them to default to the emotions of guilt, frustration or negative reasonings. This could make a person quick to react, just like I was back in my mentally clouded days. Instead, when confronted with confusions, misguided concerns, or eschewed emotions, react slowly and accordingly and at all cost stay on your path.

Just accept "to each their own," as people's actions normally reflect where they are in life. Understand that sometimes inappropriate emotions can erupt, making it look as though the person is passionate about a particular subject, yet truthfully they may not know anything about the subject at hand and it's not worth engaging in. For example, if people are caught in a lie, they may quickly develop powerful emotions as to change the direction of the conversation. The truth needs no bells or whistles; it need not sway or convince you in any way, being as it stands alone as the absolute. In retrospect, people projecting emotions like in the example above, often haven't the slightest clue about the subject matter they so passionately defend. On the other hand there are people who know an incredible amount in regard to their subjects.

Having said this, I'll share a short story further shedding light on some particulars about what the self-proclaimed know-it-alls have to say. Also in later chapters, I'll speak on the actual experts of certain subject matters, the educated, the experienced, and those certain people within your environment.

All of these, from whom we often seek answers, are sharing the best of their advice. Just know that, whomever you open up to, you need to be honest and ask yourself, do you need a good listener or are you seeking a definite answer to act upon? Remember, even friends may still divert you with the passions of their convictions, often saying things like "Well, that's just my opinion!" or maybe the fallback "It is what it is." How about that scapegoat phrase "Let go and let God"?

Not that all of these are bad advice per se, but if you're getting into the same conversational debacle after the initial advice, you might want to reevaluate your commitment to problem solving. Remember a few paragraphs ago I mentioned my personal opinion, embedded in unresolved childhood issues? By the time I was grown, again I had developed a bias against people who whisper; it may not be right in every situation, but it's a part of me I'm still working through. Ask yourself when you're in need of advice, how did your advisor come to their opinion? Even though some seem to have it all together, you never really know who a person is until they're faced with sudden adversities.

Also, I must mention those "loud" people close to you, who are not intimidated at all or afraid of what people think. These people are obviously the most compelling, just know taking on their advice is a risk reflecting their way of handling circumstances; not your own. Like in the above statement, how dare someone cause drama and trouble for those near and afar, only to suddenly say "I'm gonna let go and let God!" What's that about?

It may feel as if they are purposely going against the grain to cause friction, but that's not their intention. Unbeknownst to them, it's the agitation against the grain that causes the intended distractions suggested by the one who created the distractions in the first place. Ever notice someone getting angry because they don't know how to read?

Again, ever witness how smart people think they are in the climax of an argument? Worst yet, don't get in a conversation with someone who's intoxicated and speaking their mind on a subject like oppression, relationships or religion. Misguided people create strongholds on particular subjects just because of their perceptions, ideas, or socioeconomic upbringings. This doesn't mean they're bad people—they may have temporarily lost their path, and that is fine—but that's where the leaders by example like you come in, showing empathy, knowing people's perceptions can in fact be misconstrued.

For instance, my friend, like many others, finds it much easier to blame God for all the tragedies around the world, and in doing this provides the ability to hide behind his own denials and responsibilities.

People passionately defend political opinions too—but have you ever conversed with someone who was a fierce Republican simply because they believed it came with a certain prestige? And later you found out they were bringing in less than $40,000 annually and had no clue about the issues and policies or even who within the Republican party? How about sports—is Ohio State football better than Michigan State? Isn't this just a game?

Depending on embedded information, our opinions are simply suggestions from outside forces. And innocently enough, some opinions are brought about by ethnic backgrounds, cultural practices or traditions. Problems arise when people emphatically defend their positions, even though they don't know the actual origins of their ideas.

Only when you visualize through the eyes of the enlightened can you understand that this is far more than just a game; it's about the life and death of a person's intended journey. Just as the seasons of earth pass in due time, we all go through our cold winters and dry summers. But the bottom line is that the seasons change for the purpose of renewal. Without the waters from the melting ice, the spring would not be as bountiful, and so forth.

Our minds afford us the same process; when one season comes to pass, its sacrifice ushers in the next season to flourish. When old understandings become new, the intelligence-building process ascends to a higher level.

We were meant to grow, flourish, and transcend just as the turning of a page in a good book, that is which each page building upon the next. Also, as mentioned prior, it is my purpose to help. In doing so, I hope to call to action all whom have been exposed to a higher level of consciousness within the spirit. We have been endowed with a blessed responsibility, not a burden.

We are as one within this journey, so please use the light of your gifts to elevate the positive essence of life, as it was meant to be at this point in time. My stand is that some things are created to keep your mind cluttered, unfocused, and occupied. Without clarity, we're basically robots, programmed to do the will of the operator. If you don't believe me, that's okay—we all have our own opinions. Even though I've briefly touched on this topic, let's go over it again, as there are many different analogies embedded in this book yet to be uncovered. Take television programs, for example: the name states the intended purpose right out. It "tells" your "vision" what it wants you to see by way of "programming" the mind. Seriously, ask yourself who's making up your mind or better question who's suggesting and or persuading your actions?

In my younger years, the elderly called it the "one-eyed devil," because it looks within your home to take your mind away and replace it with the powers that be. So, again, why do advertisers spend millions upon millions of dollars every year advertising to the consciousness of you and your family? In short, they gain the essence of your brain power. Have you ever felt like you had a medical issue after being bombarded by the veritable plethora of new medicine commercials?

They implant suggestions in your mind by rattling off a multitude of conditions, and before you can blink, they slip in the side effects, which are in turn greater than the ailment—if one existed in the first place. Then they paint a beautiful picture of a person enjoying life with friends, family, or children, with the promise that their drug will heal your afflictions. Is it all really a game, or are there other forces at work? Humorously speaking, can anyone really read the small warning paragraphs some of these drug commercials flash at the bottom of the screen?

It's kind of an insult when you think about it but it's widely accepted, being most simply want relief from their symptoms, voiding the cure as an impossibility. This would be considered a form of brainwashing if it wasn't so blatant over the years. Now getting back on track we've journeyed through a few of my dreams, thought processes, and life encounters. How can this apply to helping you or someone you know break the barriers of the mind? For starters, we need to understand the purpose of issues, circumstances, and distractions, for they are not the enemy. Even though they might appear problematic or as if they were fanning the flames of evil, I promise you these inconveniences are set in place for our growth.

Think of them as steps leading to a better place, i.e. higher consciousness or enlightenment. After all, we go to school and complete one level at a time to prepare us for life; well, the same is true of the barriers in life. Use them as stepping stones to get over and ultimately ahead! Remember, most distractions are brought on by our own misconceptions, unwarranted curiosities, and short attention spans.

So when we sit and really ponder it, we can see that distractions are nothing more than small tests, set up to see how you learn, receive, and progress through the circumstances of everyday life. Furthermore when we realize in retrospect that the world isn't as terrifying as once we perceived, it frees the mind up a bit so we can work on ourselves. In other words, the less you worry about things you can't control, the more freedom your mind has to think positively, heal, resolve, and rest.

With all this being said, we can no longer blame the devil for certain issues, circumstances, or distractions—again, most being problems we've inadvertently created.

So the next time something appears to be a barrier or a trap leading to your perceived destruction, don't stress out or allow it to cause you anxiety, because we know it's just a stepping stone to a higher level. In order to move quickly past the time-consuming traps of unpleasant circumstances, we must learn to forgive swiftly, shake it off, and avoid similar situations in the future.

Just know that finding yourself is a process and in undergoing it, you'll lose who you and your friends think you are and rise as the person you were created to be. Now, on to that short story I mentioned way-earlier in the chapter, about the self-proclaimed know-it-alls and what they have to contribute compared to my purpose. I once met a man at a sports bar who claimed he knew every sports statistic regarding football. He boasted he had no real job and was divorced, but for the price of three dollars, he would prove he had unchallenged knowledge in his particular subject.

Also if he was wrong, he'd give back a total of five dollars, no questions asked. He was truly intelligent and confident in his craft, impressing the people standing around him in total amazement. When he found his way to challenge me on all things football, I immediately gave him three dollars, cleared my throat, and asked, "Where's the bathroom?"

The look of confusion seemed to distort his face as he slowly pointed in the opposite direction, I then nodded my head and walked away. The end. There are many analogies and morals within this story, and I'm proud to share it, especially since all that I have to offer, isn't as easy to talk about as some of my experiences yet to be revealed.

As for the short story, I'll say this much: there was no comparison between my so-called wisdom at seventeen years of age and his field of expertise and intelligence on football. At that specific time of our lives, we were both in need of something: he needed money, and I desperately needed to use the restroom! As I said, we're all on this journey together. No matter what phase you're in, just keep your forward progression. When you think on it, this is but one of the many examples of using forgiveness, shaking it off, or using avoidance so that you can continue on your destined path and purpose.

Remember, distractions are in place for many reasons; please remember your commitment and take the necessary steps to avoid them as you continue through your progressive journey. When the day comes and you encounter an entity all-knowing in its purpose, decide quickly if it's conducive to assisting with the overall nature of your journey.

If so, listen, open up, and share your place within the journey in order to receive a higher level of understanding. Furthermore yet again, if you encounter a being all-knowing in its purpose that is not conducive to the well-being of your overall spiritual nature, turn away swiftly!

We must avoid negative spirits with deep prejudice, lest we become trapped within a web of soul-consuming deceit. Remember, anything that guides or tempts us off our path could be detrimental to our purpose as well as what others are counting on us to provide. This is why I use what I've learned to get past circumstances otherwise thought to consume me. My hope is that we all share our experiences for the sake of raising a higher consciousness of man, while on this earth. In doing so, we'll enjoy a bit of heaven in this reality as it was meant to be since the dawn of creation.

Let's pause for a moment,

The meaning behind the title of this book;
THE CONSCIOUSNESS of MAN

"The consciousness of man depicts the complete awareness of self; mind, body and soul. It speaks upon all of mankind as a unity, equaling the sum total of our spiritual convictions."

- Reginald O'Neal Gibson

Continue Please

Hidden Chapter
The Game of the Fates

Life as we've come to know it is cluttered with many misconstrued understandings and beliefs. I've come to accept that most people, acting in the kindness of their hearts, really don't know where they stand within their created purposes. And thus they follow the insidious ways taught by those who would invest in misconstrued principles for the selfishness of personal gain.

Allowing this to manifest itself weighs heavily on the consciousness of man. When misdirection and purposeful intent are embedded, negative delusions and self-doubt tend to sidetrack our ambitions, goals, and created purposes. This is to say that most people don't realize just how important these things are. That is until a life-changing event comes along and challenges their perspectives on everything they have learned in and around our culture.

As for myself, life was continuously riddled with obstacles, barriers, and difficult circumstances, but I was able to maneuver in such a way that I arose as the victor in every mind-boggling situation. This was by no means my own cognitive doing. In every life-or-death situation that ambushed me on my path, an intercessor deep within the subconsciousness of my mind intervened; it had been patiently waiting to assist in the achievement of my created purposes.

This chapter stems from a vision within a dream I had when I was a child, presumably on my deathbed. This is difficult for me to share, revisit, or even write about. In fact till this day I have found it too cumbersome to verbalize, but I've held it in long enough. I know in my heart I've survived the trials, and I'm blessed to walk the path of enlightenment, but every day is a challenge. I am trying never to fall back but to keep growing stronger and brighter with every breath I take. This dream caused mental trauma in such a way that it's still quite frightening to think about, but it's worth sharing to confirm what we all go through at some point in our lives. The amazing thing is, the trials I went through in this dream saved me on countless occasions, especially when I was confronted with the insidiousness of corruptions, which have without doubt been manifested into the reality of our everyday lives.

It is my faith that writing this part of my experience will help people overcome the unforeseen mental barriers and battles, if ever they are challenged to the same degree as I was in my trials; so here we go, and God bless.

One night I dreamed my eyes were cloudy, thick with dust and fog. I jumped up with a savage pounding in my chest, desperately trying to wipe at my face in an attempt to clear my eyes, but my arms and hands were covered with dirt, sweat, and shards of glass. Even though I had never been to or witnessed a place like this before, something appeared oddly familiar. The back of my neck felt exposed and vulnerable, as an eerie chill seem to haunt my every movement.

No matter how hard I tried, I couldn't turn around to see what was lurking behind me. My lungs felt like burnt paper, dried and brittle, as if I were inhaling the fiery debris floating around in the thickness of the surroundings. Soon that area behind my neck felt like it was being ripped even further, exposing my back to a hideous chill slowly seeping into my body.

My entire backside felt like an exposed nerve, cold and naked. As for the front of me, I was parched and humid, void of any moisture, even sweat. It was like standing in a large furnace for quite some time, confused and in absolute terror. There was no sound in the distance, and wherever I stepped, it felt like I could fall through the crust at any moment. This place appeared to be vast, but I really couldn't tell, being as my vision was badly impaired by the thickness of the fog. I couldn't shake the feeling of abandonment in my heart; it was almost as though my Spirit's knowledge were purposely hiding. Simultaneously, other senses seemed to go haywire, like I was suffering the g-forces from a F-22 Raptor. At times I felt extremely heavy, and other times I felt like I was the victim of a centrifugal force experiment gone wrong, barely stomaching my lack of balance and direction. Yet still I pressed on, walking deeper into the darkness.

By now, I could feel the flesh of my feet ripping away from the searing heat of the ground, exposing the skeleton of my heels.

Soon after walking quite some distance, I started to hear sounds, but it was the clacking of my bones walking on the hard surface, as now the flesh was completely torn from the soles of my feet. Nevertheless, I was compelled to continue walking, fearing that what was behind me was getting closer. Dizziness set in, as well as heat exhaustion, but that was the least of my worries, so forward I walked.

That is until I bumped into something extremely frigid. My eyes still clouded, I could barely make sense of what was right in front of me, but that didn't stop my soul driven push. Soon after, something vaguely appeared in front of me. Needing desperately to find something tangible so I could make sense of things, I decided to stretch my arms forward and lay my hands upon it, and it materialized as a flat surface. Instantaneously immense pain shot through my hands and arms onto my chest; immediately I yanked back. It was like something snatched at me, clawing downward into my chest as if desperately searching for something hidden deep within my flesh.

The agony was horrific as intense pain resonated throughout my body. At this moment the dense fog suddenly scaled back, but just enough to reveal a table; only the fog remained hauntingly at the table's edge. As the fog receded to its side, I noticed the center of the table revealing what appeared to be a portal to another realm continuously folding within itself. This portal was of the blackest matter I've ever seen, difficult and blinding to look upon.

For a moment, I was able to witness the magnitude of its force being so powerful that it absorbed any fragments of light or matter within its surroundings. This place in which I stood felt like a sealed container but without walls, constantly moving and shifting within its own density of greenish-black smoke. At this point I felt the energy being sucked from my eyes, so I calmed myself and focused my sight away from the pull of the table.

Still, visibility was increasingly difficult—that is, until I noticed a change from the other side. Piercing through the density of the fog came a pair of white gloves. They motioned for me to come closer, to look within the blackness of the table, but I remained steadfast.

At this point, again something appeared vaguely familiar. It was as if I had traveled to a similar place, but this place was too frightening to ever forget; I felt completely alone. Also on top of the fear of abandonment it inspired, this place was made of darkness, filled with unrest and deceit. Now trying to look deeper, I couldn't make out the form behind the gloves, being as the fog cloaked its every movement as though it were attached to the form's body.

Soon the gloves moved frantically back and forth, as if to fan the smoke away and reveal its true form. Something was happening, something very harmful; it was then when my soul confirmed this wasn't a dream! Upon this realization, something burst forward from deep within my spirit. A seed had opened, and memories swiftly started to rush toward my despair; I was being tested.

Now I understood the gloves' gestures of grace and dance swaying back and forth—they were seeking agreement. Had I actually believed it was trying to fan away the fog to reveal its true image, it would have entered me into this agreement. Upon acceptance, this would have immediately collected my spirit into the void of the table; this was the first attack, the attack of the mind. As memories emerged for my defense, a multitude of voices simultaneously spoke from behind the fog.

"Hello," they said, but I did not answer.

"Hello?" Again and again the voices spoke, as they channeled down to one slow, haunting tone. It was obvious to me that this voice was searching to calibrate itself with my mental process, but I remained still with peace. As gentle as the voice tried to be after its initial introduction, its vibration resonated sickness deep within my stomach. It was as if intuitions and confidence were savagely being suctioned from my gut.

"Wonderful!" The fog boasted as it sang in delight, leaving the foulest of smells all around me. "You've found your way through the darkness; this means you're quite special.

If you were truly lost, you would have been savagely drawn within the beauty of the all-giving table. To chance the journey without a path reveals greatness within you!" "Peace, be still," my heart temporarily uncloaked itself to whisper, then again retreated somewhere deep within my soul.

At this point, the fog's gloves danced with every syllable it spoke. "Rest," it said, as the foul-mouthed entity solidified a chair from the smoke behind me.

"It's your destiny to be rewarded with the game of the fates. For you to have journeyed this far, your wisdom must have been molded within the spirits of war." At this moment another seed from within was revealed. "Disregard embellishment; it will manifest the false light of conceit and will collect you within the void."

Then the gloves gestured to a game as it rose from the darkness of the table. Its form was that of a spectacular chess board. The white squares were like vast waterfalls from different worlds flowing endlessly into the game. Between these squares remained the blackness of the void, resembling galaxies being engulfed into an abyss.

"Choose," the fog patiently said, as the most brilliant of chess pieces fell from its gloves. The whitest of white and the blackest of black characters spilled upon the board, hovering with the anticipation of being touched. The white pieces were the images of beautiful women positioned in the form of praise and worship, while the black pieces were intricately carved men, bent over, bearing the weight of many large but differently shaped stones upon their backs.

Again I was being tempted, but now it was by intrigue, as the tone of the voice suddenly started to change. This time it became the many voices of women, pleading seductively from the mouths of the white chess pieces.

Still, I remained not swayed by the puppeteer's manipulation of the chessboard, being as his foul odor became more and more evident with every word spoken.

"Play me please; play me now," the women began to beg. "Save us, save us please!" I remained quiet. "Save her, you fool, and hurry, do it now!" the black chess pieces screamed, in excruciating pain while being crushed slowly by the weight upon their backs. Still I resisted, as the sounds of bickering resonated from the mouths of the women chess pieces. Moment later they dropped their arms from frozen praise and slowly turned with hideous eyes staring right at me.

Haunting chills began to rise throughout my stomach and back, then up to my throat. It felt like I was being strangled and scratched by the many hands of the women figures, but I remained still. "Save us!" again and again, as their voices grew louder, morphing into the screeching sounds of metal scraping down a chalkboard.

"Bastard! You bastard!" the voices screamed. "You've killed me, you bastard, you've killed us all!" As they sang a horrible song of death and profanity, they were tearing off their skin, savagely biting and killing each other with long fanged teeth. Soon the screams of agony and terror started to fade into the faint whimpering of cries slowly dying out. At this point I stood frozen in shock as their blood flowed past the bodies of the crushed men and off the board, collecting into the abyss of the table. Then there was silence, absolutely no movement at all.

Until I moved to take a step forward, trying desperately to understand what just happened. Then everything, especially the ground upon which I stood, shook violently as though the weight of a planet had collapsed within itself.

I then felt that enormous presence of vile wickedness from behind me, slowly moving closer to uncover any weaknesses I allowed to coddle my mind. I could sense the darkness increasingly growing with anger and hatred from my presence in this realm. During the violent quake of the crust, I could feel a shift in angle, as if I were falling backward yet standing perfectly still.

Now a different voice spoke, far more sinister than anything I'd heard in this place. Its voice spoke directly to my mind, and I could feel it was confused and desperately searching for something as well. "I can feel the weak flicker of light dying out in your decaying flesh, begging to be consumed," the being said, creeping more slowly in my direction.

"You can try to hide to no avail; I can smell the remnants of blood in your desiccated body; look to me child, and be taken from this place." I tried once again to remain motionless, but I was too late, it was locked onto my position. What made it worse was I still couldn't turn to see what was behind. Yet something it said struck me. It said I was "of light," and that resonated as familiar in my consciousness. Only still, I just wanted to bring peace to my mind, silencing any thoughts or fears. All I knew was that I was afraid, vulnerable, and in dread of this place. The feeling of being paralyzed was growing immensely as I started to visualize something horrifically unexplainable coming at me from behind.

Also, as I mentioned, the shift in gravity made it feel as if I were falling backward, and this meant that the weight of my body appeared to be going in the direction of the being. Of course this was of no matter; it was coming regardless, and its focus was directly on me.

My eyes were still closed as if the deep sleep of a coma had taken over me, and my focus was on trying to ignore the crackling of hot breath now pushing against my back. I felt imminent dread and despair as the dark image slowly emerged from the left side of my shoulder. I could tell the being originally had no form, but it soon started to transform into a more humanlike appearance. The form continued to shift until it was a large, dark, triangular blob, hunched over, with a head a decrepit mixture of man and wild boar. Where its eyes scrutinized my body, it seared me with intense pain. Desperately I concentrated to close myself off once again, but the searing focus of this being was too close.

Its burning gaze was smoldering up the center of my back, across my chest, and upward past my cheek. I knew at this time that its intent was to devour my soul and assume control of the vessel within my mind. Frantic, I tried to run, but there was nowhere to go. The best I could do was slip off the bones of my feet, helplessly landing on my knees in child's pose. I shivered as I looked up, face burning with the fire, then on to the taste of my own flesh, shooting vomit violently from my mouth. I couldn't utter a word, not even in pain, but soon I remembered something I had learned in a different place; a sound.

The sound of a name, this name was so powerful, no breath could hold its weight, but all one would have to do is think it. Trying to verbalize it in our earthly realm, it would sound like *Yahweh*, but in the spirit form of the word, the sound is of unimaginably pure energy, immense, as the tone could be heard across all the realms and universes, resonating more powerfully than any form of matter humans could imagine. And it was shown to me, "Just listen. As it was spoken since the dawn of time, this name resides, omnipotent, never to end."

"Yahweh!" I thought, "I submit my soul only to you—do with it as you will." Then I heard another voice, far different from the presence of the seed, revealed at particular times from within. "Open!" I heard, and a great flow of peace broke from a dam, pouring the coolness of fresh water to quench my burning soul.

Also the presence of the seed spoke, saying, "Reggie, get up! You have something to do!" I then remembered my time journeying, being tempered within its bosom. This was when I was just a child, clinging onto dear life while in the hospital. "Look once again, through your mind's eye." An ability revealed to me in another time swiftly came to my aid. I could now see, even when my eyes were burned past recognition, and my soul tormented.

Yet upon this vision, things swiftly changed back to the original place of fog. There I stood once again, right before I'd reached out and touched that frigid table.

Only this time I withdrew from the need to curiously stretch my hand out in aimless wonder. Instead, at this moment I chose to simply stand still. "Well played!" the fog said, as I placed my hands back down to my sides. Something was wrong; the fog seemed to stare at me in confusion, and then it swiftly approached my face, breathing erratically. "Did you speak to my father?" it demanded in a tense, bemused tone. Again, "Did you see my father?" screamed the fog as it cursed, spewing atrocities of anger.

"You smell of hate; how is this possible? Reach out to me!" the fog yelled in a tremendous tone. Then it went swiftly back to silence, but only for a moment. I then heard the innocent sound of a boy whimpering, as though he were frightened and scared to speak. "Sir, where's my mother?" he asked in the most innocent child's voice. I heard it again.

"Sir, I can't see her! I can't see her! I can't find my mother; did you kill her? Where's my mother? I can't see her—is that her? I can't see her; can you help me?" At this moment I started to feel uneasy. I was losing my strength, and even though my eyes were seared, again I could feel the blackness from the void pulling energy from my eye sockets.

The child spoke again, but this time in a playfully teasing tone. "Guess what, sir?" the child's voice whispered as it got closer to my ear. "I got a secret!" The little voice started to sing aloud, playfully as the fog moved even closer. "I hate you!" the voice screamed loudly, as the gloves spread far apart and above, as if they belonged to a terrifying giant.

"I've always hated you! You're nothing!" it shouted again, and again. Repetitively the fog taunted, as it was regurgitating the contents of what appeared to be human organs from its belly.

"You're nothing, nothing!" it was repeating again and again, throwing up more and more pestilence and blood. At this point I was trying not to slip off the bones of my feet, being I was now standing in the burning acidic contents of its spewed innards. "Why don't you breathe, you bastard? Your chest hasn't risen in this realm! Your heart has no beat—where is the breath of life within you?" The fog screamed while frantically moving about, "Why haven't you taken one breath? What are you!?" I replied not, for this was my last test, the test of will. By now the memories from the seed within me had been manifested to their fullest potential. I now clearly remembered: I once was tempered within the bosom of the Holy Spirit. In this place it was impressed upon my soul that I need not breathe if I ever lost my way. Also, I was told that the breath of life leads directly to the heart's field of energy. This is why we should never become scornful, lest our nostrils burn closed, severing the channels between the anointed realms.

While in the bosom of the unfathomable wisdom, I only took one breath that lasted for over seven months. As my teachings ended, I released that breath and awoke within the earth. Also I was taught that if I ever encountered such a realm, to close my eyes so as to reveal true sight from within. Then I should put my right hand flat under my heart and the left hand open under my neck, cupping it firmly.

Next I should lean my head down over my hand and feel my heartbeat, then rest, not to even mumble a word, and become absent of all thought. This would allow the pulse to reconnect with the heart and channel through the vessel of my clarified mind. In doing this, I was instantaneously pulled from the place of despair.

This dream changed me. It allowed me to understand life in a way that is difficult to relay or explain because of the accepted teachings of this world. Understand, all is known through the spirit of justice. Even all of those whom we thought had been erased from history, murdered without evidence of their bodies and presumed never to be found—the names, family looms, and cultures of these people still remain, constant within the subconscious of man.

They are still fulfilling the covenant of their creation and sharing wisdom with the worthy and enlightened. Know that these souls are intricately weaved into the fabric of our consciousness, speaking and teaching through the realms of truth and knowledge, assisting as they were originally created to. Acknowledge that what we perceive as death on earth is only the beginning of something far more important.

Please understand when the wickedness of the world's strongholds attack, with atrocities intent on devouring you, be still, listen to your heart, and trust that it holds the embedded wisdom for your survival. Remember, do not conform to the false perceptions of this reality, and by all means do not get distracted, because your blessed destiny is within your reach.

Know that most assume a dream is just a dream, but only when you reach mental clarity can you discover what dreams and visions are truly about.

Upon this understanding, you can wield a certain power acquired from the ancient knowledge, as I and many others within this world do. Seek for yourself, but know that this requires that you take the journey. When ready, prepare yourself for the battles and become overly abundant for the purposes of good. Lastly, one more essential point: if you accept the journey, acknowledge the darkness with enlightenment and continue past this place.

It's imperative to your reality, as well as the reality of others around you, that you stay focused. Remember when traveling, refrain from any form of hesitation while passing through the darkness, for it holds many distractions set to take control of your vessel, which is needed for you to cross back over into this world; this needs to not happen; Peace be within your journey.

Chapter 6
The Pulse of the Mountain

Looking back on my childhood, it seems like I was able to create my own self-fulfilling reality, not for attention's sake, but again to save the world as I thought it to be. The problem was, the more I explored or envisioned my adventures and battles, the more I inadvertently attracted trials and tribulations within my reality. Was this the law of attraction making itself known in my life? If so, that was not my intended goal.

Nevertheless, these self-fulfilling prophecies paved the foundation for the spiritual battles I would encounter later on in my journey as a young adult. The one thing I can say about the acceptance of such responsibility is that our spirits can free themselves from the barriers, depression, and fears buried deep within the mind. God's word can be the light that reflects upon your heart in its darkest hour, as it did mine. The darkness was never to bind us again before the dawning of our paths. The other understanding I acquired out of my early struggles was that my knowledge of spiritual battles would be of great benefit to the multitude of people lost within a system of spiritual complacency. I knew that my acquired knowledge of selflessness could be an asset to all who wanted to listen, if it was sought out. As far as being anointed to speak, that wasn't my calling, at least not at that time. My calling was to survive the turmoil of life and take note while leading by example, and I suspect yours is as well.

Only the human mind, more specifically the consciousness of the mind, has been programmed with misinformation, making it difficult to understand true depth. This breeds barriers and accepted boundaries of fear, guilt, and lack of responsibility. One cannot achieve peace or even truth in knowledge without the balance of the mind-body-spirit trinity, but most create fear out of the very laws created to break these bonds. It's simple; we were created with an infinite power deep within our spirit and embedded within this power is the freedom of will; only the sin within the chosen will of humankind causes people to turn from the laws that unlock the infinite possibilities of life.

The connection of the heart and spirit is cluttered because of the selfish manifestations embedded within the channels of the mind. Ever heard someone say, "sound mind and spirit," or "being of sound mind and body"? Ask yourself what is meant by the word sound. Is it a form of foundation meant to uphold the body and translate communication within the spirit? If so, foundation created by what substance and from what origin? Is the articulation of hearing involved? If so, who's speaking? Is the ear involved with the process of interpreting vibrations into sound and sound into words, or does the perception of the mind trump the process? If so, how does your knowledge interpret these words into meaning with true understanding? If you received the true interpretation, the questions still remain: Where did the sound originate, and would you be obedient to its teachings?

Furthermore, are our understandings and interpretations of its meaning received and reciprocated? If and when this is so, do you have the ability to translate the knowledge for others? Ask yourself what you would do with its purpose. Even more, can we abide by this life-fulfilling balance? One example of this process comes to mind in this physical realm: the anointed translations of people who speak in tongues! This exchange develops within the spirit by reciprocal balance between the heavens and earth. It was true when I was being healed within the bosom of the Holy Spirit, and to a select few remains true within our society.

During my first encounter with the Holy Spirit, it was explained to me that if I were to try and speak in his realm, it would be like birds chirping in the morning. So when someone speaks in tongues in this reality, it sounds just as different as well. Also, I remember I wasn't breathing as I would normally breathe, and it was shared with me that oxygen as I knew it was different in the spirit realm. Instead of using oxygen, there, our entire bodies pulsate energy shared with all in existence, past and present, as a form of stored energy, like the wind, water, soil, and even gravity. For instance, every cycle of breath I used on earth was the equivalent to one pulse of shared energy over the course of seven months within his presence.

In this realm, flesh doesn't exist, only the form of energy shaped by the Spirit. So without the limits of the body, the mind can fully experience the essence of heaven, as long as corruption hasn't manifested doubt, guilt, or even the acceptance of death. Once you let go of these insecurities within your mind, you can achieve the path of righteousness.

In revisiting my encounter within a dream, one evening I was brought back to a spiritual realm. I remembered sitting with my elbows resting on my knees, crossed legs and totally relaxed. I was simultaneously atop the peak of a mountain, very close to the hospital building's ledge from another time. I could see what appeared to be two worlds at once because time was no longer linear. The mountain was thick with lush, green grass in my mind's eye. The others were looking down the edge of the building. The Spirit explained I was seeing past and present in the moment of now.

The spirit impressed upon me that the now was timeless, and if I could see through my mind with clarity, I could travel the channels of the now at will within the lure of my heart. Where the building now stood had once been a beautiful mountain; it resided within eyesight of a great river that split the land of my ancestors' village.

I replied, "My ancestors? I'm Native American?" The Spirit said, "We are all within the now, the land, waters and air," and before I could think to ask I was shown a beautiful vision.

On a special night of the feast, the Blackfoot tribe celebrated a worthy cause: a new spirit was born, yielding the powers to heal and fill the air with sweet aromatics. The sky was royal blue, and the air was crisp to the nostrils, but suddenly the chief stopped the celebration and gazed at the stars. Soon her eyes glowed bright as she noticed a moving shadow across the surface of the moon.

Something different was in the sky that night; it turned out to be that a fallen star was off course and was en route to hitting the earth.

Swiftly the chief cut a part of her hair and tossed it into the fire; the incense from the flame rose, sought out six villagers, and entered their nostrils. Then the chosen villagers fell where they stood and started to violently shake. Moments later they arose, growing simultaneously from their natural heights to what seemed to be two or three stories tall. Without any directions given, every villager was of one accord, they stood firm stretching out their arms while firmly placing their hands on the hearts of every man, woman, and child. From my view above, the tribe formed what was revealed to be a massive human dream catcher, perfectly centered around their leader.

As the chief sat within the circle, she held the newborn spirit closely to her breast and covered the baby with her flowing hair. At this time, the ground began to glow a brilliant green as she started to sing the most beautiful lullaby. I remembered how her voice echoed as she sang to all the animals and spirits within nature, forming an outer circle running counter-clockwise around the standing tribal people. Soon the drums started to beat as her body rose high above the village, levitating in midair while protecting baby.

Then the ground trembled as the six giant villagers ran swiftly in the direction of the moon, miles away, then stopped abruptly as they witnessed a rapid wall of water coming toward them, devastating everything in its path.

The giant warriors knelt down and grabbed deep within the soil of the earth, pulling upward and stretching its roots like an enormous quilt, and then together they swiftly ran back, stretching this massive land of trees and grass with them.

Overwhelmed, I felt like I was having an out-of-body experience of pure anxiety, yet I was able to nervously take it all in. "Listen," the Holy Spirit said. "Listen for the origin of the heartbeat." Soon the giants were rapidly approaching the village. It felt like an earthquake was hitting as I watched the massive wall of water and devastation on the heels of the dashing giants. Swiftly, as the giants entered the edge of the village, they jumped high into the air, above and over the arisen chief, and blanketed themselves and the village as they fell within the land. Instantaneously the waters hit, crashing against the covered mountain village, flowing around its massive surface. Soon, within the darkness of the mountain, a fire was lit and the drum started to beat once again. Where the stars used to cover the night sky, were now eagles flying between the richness and beauty of green grass and mighty trees.

The blanketed land protected her village from the destructive force of the waters; in this the creation of the lush green mountain came to pass. On nights of full moon and royal blue skies, a mind of true clarity can feel the pulse of the tribe's worship resonating throughout the land. This is where, if needed, healing takes place as the faint sounds of beating drums lead the seekers of enlightenment throughout the sacred land.

This was the mountain the Holy Spirit and I sat upon in the past realm, feeling the pulse of the drums as the ceremony of life continued to heal the weak through the nourishment of Earth's soil. He told me, "Nothing truly perishes, all is eternal, and all is now continuously transitioning from one place in time to another."

Since, I've come to realize that the acorn holds great power; to bury it doesn't mean ending its life cycle but beginning its purpose. Thus the cycle of the mighty oak tree remains constant and never-ending. Envision with me following another's footprints throughout the land, on a path left by the covenant of the creator, in which we have a guide for traveling through the darkness and into the light. Our minds are the footprints within this journey; unclutter this path, and we possess the ability to travel either direction. But again know what is considered darkness or death has its purpose, being as it is preceded by the ever-flowing light of life. This can be understood too in the analogy of when the child leaves the mother's body. Up until this point, the child only knew its mother's womb, liquid filled its lungs with life-giving nutrients, and its warmth pulsated with the heart of its mother. Imagine the feeling of suddenly being birthed into this cold world. Some would compare this transition to the abrupt end of their lives, but let's ponder this a bit: just like the burial of the acorn, is this life's end, or is it the beginning of a much greater purpose? It depends on whose perspective you take. If looking from God's perspective, you'd understand the transitions of life as a part of its meaning and purpose, but if you look at it from humankind's perspective, you might thoughtlessly question what type of god would allow death within the world.

It often amazes me how some people fear death but choose not to live life as it was meant to be lived. This reminds me of when I was asked by a stranger in passing, "What's the purpose of life?" I gave a quick response: "To live it!" But what does that mean to people if they don't know what living life is? This continuously brings me back to why we should clear the mind as to see what's really in front of us: life existing all around us. Enjoy it.

Understand nothing really dies; it only transcends. But in the consciousness of man, most fear death because of the unknown and because of embedded guilt. Often we're led off our path, temporarily forgetting the purpose of our creation, and truthfully there is no mystery as to why: we're simply busy with the continuous bombardment of "stuff," and stuff accumulates cluttering the mind. So, in turn, at some point in our lives we decide to gather up as much physical stuff as possible, to balance out the weight of our consciousness. This is why most eventually seek the path of "enlightenment."

Upon finding this path, the weight is lifted from our minds, and in accomplishing this lift, we can finally think. Upon thinking, we can transcend, and when we transcend, we are no longer held by the bonds or weight of this world. Just remember that coveting and trying to accumulate all that this world has to offer comes with a price, and since we can't take our degrees, trophies, and material belongings with us, we might want to follow the footsteps of our intended path so as to ascend into the light of God's original purpose.

Chapter 7
The Awakening

Hopefully by now you've come to the realization that something remarkable awaits your acknowledgment. Just know that all is within your reach when you finally take that leap of faith, trusting fully in your heart. Just remember: this takes place after the awakening. I know it's hard for most to accept the order of things, but trust that it's well worth your wait in patience, forgiveness, and commitment. It is my hope that I've reminded you of the knowledge already shared with you within your dreams, visions, and experiences, and by far more knowledgeable people who have spoken beforehand. Just know that I'm trying to do my part by fanning the favorable winds of change in your direction.

  Please do not dismiss the content of this book as merely chance, coincidence, or even curiosity, and please forgive my ignorance on particular subjects, being as I'm sharing information as it was given as a continuously learning process through my walk of the enlightenment. Nothing we do is perfect, but when the seeds of knowledge become mature, looking back on the little things reminds us to remain humble. So, to all: instead of holding onto your experiences, I want you to take a chance, another leap of faith, and as I did, to remind others and light up the paths of many. Just know the best we can do is assist each other while on the journey. Questions, questions, questions, brought on to challenge you to connect the dots—I get it, but please be patient, all *Analogies* will be *revealed*.

Many people more intellectual, clever, and sensitive than I, may now be speaking against all that I've written thus far. Notice I used *thus* instead of the word *so* at the end of my last sentence? This is because the mind reacts to the thought process, body movement, and language of a character because of its perceived image. In other words, I inadvertently thought about the intellectual critics, sharp-witted and opinionated, reviewing my words and the structure of this book and immediately felt like I should sound like what I believe they sound like—that is, using the word *thus* in the sentence. Please understand I didn't do that on purpose; it was the reaction of my mind when I envisioned the scrutiny of some in the process of forcing themselves through this book.

Here's what I'm getting at: all minds have been programmed to a certain degree, but there comes a time when a question or thought process challenges the system. These challenges can go either way; in my case, I believe what I've been exposed was sufficient for me to have come to some thought-provoking meanings. For many others, understanding what I write may have immediately came to a halt because of the recurring thought "Where's this guy's proof, facts, and references?" I get it—some need evidence to validate current or new information. The only issue is, even though previous literature is often cited as evidence or fact, that is: knowledge stood upon and translated throughout the history of books, scrolls or sanskrit, at some point received their information from somewhere. Some sort of wisdom shared as an original source of purity as to guide and preserve the purpose of life. With this understanding, maybe one can see that what we know as the bible still has information or mysteries ready to be acknowledge.

Maybe more mind boggling, who's to say the bible isn't still being written and recorded as to course correct any misinformation purposely created to lead future generations farther away from truth with the stories of our origins, powers within this world an or the meaning of life? Moreover, know that such knowledge may not be converted through the tainted hands of many but rather within the conscious spirit of all. This is when I write, I write upon the confirmations that most have already been instilled with a glimmer within their heartfelt intuition.

My hope is that I've struck a cord of insight reminding you that we are in fact as one in consciousness, if so ask yourself have I said anything that caused you to think "hey! I had a feeling, dream, vision or peace about what this author is saying." If not that's fine, we all have our opinions as well as travel the paths at different paces.

Let's look at it from a slightly different angle, every brick laid such as within the great pyramid of Giza is considered essential, from the bottom to the top. In realizing this, know that collectively, every brick is considered the sum total of one great pyramid, as being one.

Here's my point: is the integrity of the very first brick laid, more important than the last brick placed upon the pyramid's completion?

The answer is no, especially since the composition and integrity of the brick is exact in the purity of its elemental origin. Now imagine if even one brick was not of the same strength and integrity, it could cause a crack in the foundation. In this circumstance, it could lead to a chain reaction eventually causing the foundation to crumble upon itself. Understand that the crack as a result of insufficient integrity can be closely related to a crack in information throughout mankind. Purposely and falsely translated to lead and misguide a foundation of truth and wisdom to crumble upon the weight of misguided consciousness.

In this, the purity of source or reference, whether old or new, remains consistent to the best of our knowledge, being as it originated from somewhere in its God given creative origin of truth. This is why upon relieving our overly weighted minds from stress, clutter and distractions can we reach an enlightened sense of self and mindfulness. Awakening as the higher humans within life leading by example to course correct the righteous from misguided paths. This is who we are, This is what is meant for us to do, no matter what worldly ailments, ethnic race or character of class you've been given. A higher calling of purpose remains within you, soon to be awaken when least expected.

In my case, I assert that my source is as pure as that of the knowledgeable scholars, spiritual leaders, and teachers of truth that had communion within the realms of higher consciousness.

If the actions of my character or word within my honor are not enough, that's fine—we all have our opinions—but know that truth is truth without any bells or whistles, and I'm making an effort to simply remind you of some special qualities yet to be revealed; that exists in the both of us.

Just know, refusing to be an accepting person could cause a serious barrier for those who prize "facts" more than the idea of questioning their assumptions or intuitions about reality. Sometimes a breakthrough is so close we turn away too soon, thinking it will never come to pass! Also, getting back to my integrity, some may argue that if my information isn't based off tangible evidence or a PhD, then why should they believe in what I have written? Furthermore, if anyone could write whatever they wanted and then call themselves authors, this world would be filled with even more unsubstantiated facts, perceptions, and personal opinions. Know that this is true, but we live in a mass-writing world where everyone wants to add their knowledge or views to the stream. The scary possibility is, one day hundreds of years from now, a person may pick up a book and base his or her entire philosophy on the writings of another's false representation of a worthy cause and in doing so become an expert on a subject that holds no worth, justice or honor for the betterment of humanity. This is why I write in the spirit, for truth will always be confirmed; timeless in its origin. Again, my point: there is a lot of not-so-great literature in the world, but no more than there is misinformation purposely printed or generated to control, persuade, or influence a generation for someone's own self-fulfilling or cultural purposes. So here's a quick check on the truth of a person's character, are they happy?

Are they humbly fulfilling the purpose of life in joy and abundance? Remember, it's not the wealth of a person's financial assets that reflect truth or worth for that matter, but rather the fundamental balance of peace within themselves as well as the people around them.

This brings me back to the awakening of a thought process. The system is setup to make a person "believe" as well as "ignore." For instance, in a court of law, there is always an expert who comes to speak on the topic—and then afterward, another expert from the opposite side introduces factually based evidence to persuade the jury, with just as many degrees, books, and experiences as the other expert. How can there be two experts adamantly defending different viewpoints on the same subject?

This is not to say the experts are wrong; just know that "to each their own" applies in regard to the core truth of their knowledge. Some sources truly are better than others, and I'd much rather trust my doctor than a remedy on a social media post, but as I said, in a court of law, someone's hoping that the information being provided is based off of core values and truths. Here's my rule of thumb for evaluating the circumstances when someone is trying to pursue or otherwise convince me. First, why am I the target of their interest? Second, am I actually lusting or putting myself in the position to be taken advantage of? Third, what would I gain or lose by being persuaded? And last, what does this person gain out of convincing me to change my mind or the direction of my focused path?

Just so you know, I don't particularly care to be convinced—it's almost up there with how I feel about people whispering in my ear—which is why this book isn't littered with references from the experts, or tons of quotes from famous authors and reference books. I don't want to vicariously ride on the backs of successful others to gain your trust.

I realize that putting the words like *Dr.* or *best seller!* on the cover or even coming up with a catchy subtitle like *7 Steps to Guarantee Wealth in 30 Days!* would sell more books, but as I see it, the truth and heartfelt honesty will reach the audience's inner selves. I know that providing evidence to back up what I'm writing is the norm, but I'm asking you to remember that the truth is deep down, already spoken within your heart. This is how you know that my experiences are not offshoots of another's ideas or, worse yet, based off someone else's embellished stories from years past, accepted and agreed upon as facts in today's world.

A lie is a lie even if a thousand years have passed, and also just because a million people say something is right doesn't mean it's right. This is why it takes more than zippy words, a flashy character, or a previously published book or two to convince me of a truth, especially if a person bases their life's study and expertise off another's written work.

I often agree with the importance of citations and proof, but sometimes it's imperative to check the original writer's purpose for there written work. Were they inspired by the works cited from another authors' opinions or spiritual guidance, either way you hold what is necessary to decipher the truth.

Note this is true for all people of spoken wisdom or knowledge within the institutions of learning and education. All of whom, who's assumed the responsibility as leaders amongst the masses; from lawmakers, religious leaders, presidents to teachers in schools and home, all sources should be validated with confirmations of truth within the results of their actions and as evidence of the theoretical knowledge.

For example, are you reading something based off a political agenda back in the 1700s? Has the author over time simply changed the manuscript to fit a new agenda? My point is that miseducation is real, and for the awakening to take hold, we must find away to tunnel through the clutter. Upon this taking place, the mind will operate at a level where all truth is shared without boundaries in time or space. Here's an example of fear-based misinformation.

Since the time Christ spoke that he'll come back within the clouds, a multitude of information, ideas, and images were created to convince our world that anything that enters our atmosphere must be an alien monster trying to take over our planet. This is to induce fear and create disbelief with our teachings. It kind of makes you wonder how we will be received when we finally find a planet we could cohabit. Will we be considerate to the new planet or as malicious as our past history has shown us to be?

I know, that's all opinion, but know that the dream I shared about the tribe and its chief was written hundreds of years ago, thought never to be read, acknowledged, or shared again.

It was shown to me that the written language of this story was burned with the holder of many stories of purpose and traditions, murdered in a wicked attempt to keep truth from flowing peacefully throughout the lands.

As mentioned, this knowledge by all accounts was thought to be buried and washed away, lost forever by devious intentions, but it was given to me and countless others by way of visions to acknowledge as truth. This truth challenges the mind to seek understanding, provoke wonder, and finally awaken. In this, the balance will be established and we will once again have powers to change the corrupted minds, body, spirit and reality, by sharing within the given rights of heaven upon earth.

This chapter is devoted to the awakening, to how you or someone you know can tangibly get on course toward the enlightened path. I'm not trying to convince but rather remind you of your intended journey, the one you've already dreamed of or felt in your gut a majority of your life.

If you've committed yourself to reading this far, it could only be for one of several reasons. You know these reasons for yourselves, so if they remain positive, I want to say thank you and please continue to trust your heart, not your mind, not just yet. If you've read this far for the purposes of negative resolve, I want to say thank you as well for allowing me to enter your consciousness. In doing so, bringing awareness as to what your true character is; by way of the law of polarity I have no doubt we'll physically meet throughout the journey of this walk.

Again, please remember to not discount our interaction as a coincidence; if you have been brought this way, exploring the various parts of my journey is essential. I've simply chosen this method to communicate awareness in the confusion of the embedded mind. You and many others may have expressed your spiritual awareness through paintings, poems, sculptures, music, and dance to name a few. Just know that I accept you, I see you, feel you, and acknowledge your blessed higher vibrational energy.

By now many could be asking themselves, "How does all this translate to me?" Understand that my path may not be exactly the path you're on, but the wisdom gained through trials and experiences are the same, no matter who you are.

In other words, you can acquire knowledge from my trials and confirm what's already been seeded within your soul by your experiences. With this knowledge, you can become free of the obstacles that have been set in life to continuously misguide you or others near. So let's start the process of enlightenment by first attempting to adapt to the environment we are accustomed to and hopefully find a more practical way to the path.

This is just in case you haven't removed enough clutter to encountered spiritual elements to help guide your way, or in case you haven't had enough life-and-death experiences to enlighten your reality. Know that these spiritual elements have influenced you from birth, but often we ignore their power because of our own self-doubt. At a glance, it may seem simple, but trust in the process, knowing this will be the foundation toward your success and blessed legacy.

The initial process begins with understanding the difference between sleep and rest; learning to rest will be the first step to your awakening. When you lie down to rest at the end of your day, take time to reflect before you fall asleep. Realize you've accomplished a day worthwhile and that your rest is a special time in which you can heal and reconnect with yourself.

Acknowledging this moment is imperative to the revitalization of your temple. Moreover, as you become aware of them, you'll naturally course-correct any unmerited emotional or physical misdirections. Furthermore, this helps remove any barriers not intended for the prosperity of your future, allowing for the clarity and forward movement of your created purpose.

It's my promise to help guide you through the manifestations of troubles within your environment, so please remember the importance of the small steps upon which a solid foundation is to be created, steps such as establishing a routine for relaxation before your actual rest within the night. Many people assume that upon their lying down at night, the journey of the day's adventures are over, but I'd like to submit a different understanding.

Maybe the true journey is just beginning, and maybe the real struggle lies in the unconsciousness of your mind, and now how you've led your day will provide you with the strength to guide you through the spiritual battle at night. Ever wondered why you've slept for hours just to feel physically exhausted the next morning? Or why you tossed and turned throughout the night when you weren't aware of any problems lurking to cause unrest?

Maybe you were struggling with a decision or an unresolved matter from the previous day, or maybe you've allowed guilt, confusions, or unforgiveness to create a barrier that your consciousness wrestled with amidst the missed opportunity of closure. This is where the intentional positive reflection on your day is a must; you can control how you receive the input and, if done correctly, this could enhance your level of triumph within your day-to-day battles. Please accept that for every issue, circumstance, or problematic discussion, a barrier is created; yet we deal with these by accepting the day-to-day bombardment of our consciousness. A key factor when dealing with your thought processes is understanding that your mind is continuously programmed by misinformation, self-imposed worries, and autosuggestions.

Disregarding these suggestions as a viable threat could fuel the flame of the enemy from within, wreaking havoc and causing emotional turmoil. If not effectively countered by disengaging from the onslaught of manifested fears, the aftereffect will be an imbalance between body and spirit. The imbalance of which I speak is the opposing forces between the mind and the physical exhaustion of the body, resulting in stress. The accumulation of stress before sleep will disrupt the revitalization and healing capabilities within the body at rest. It is in this rest that you'll build the mental energy to discontinue following a directionless path and arise empowered with the ability to recreate your life in abundance.

Accept the fact that you can manifest this abundance at will, simply by speaking it into your life. This power is intricately woven into the very fabric of your being, your happiness, and your purpose.

This ability is yours to call upon. Start to visualize the analogies shared throughout this book, and you may find the similarities of our spirits confirming each other in truth. Moreover, don't allow the perception of fear to immobilize your thought process; some barriers are self-induced by the learned behaviors of contentment through association. Using the key principles to avoid the trap of deceptions will lead to understandings that provide the momentum for continued travel deeper into the uncharted paths of your mental clarity. First comes the realization of who the enemy is and what its intended purpose is; thereafter come the principles to follow. This will gradually lead you out of the art of existing in a life of uncertainty and false contentment. Acknowledging the fact that your life is affected by your perceptions, it is within the limits of your mind to become free of the distractions that obstruct your focus. Having this knowledge affords you the ability to deal with yourself as well as break down the barriers manifested deep within your mind.

Here's where the battle is fought; this is the grounds upon which your true foundation, character, and personality are built. If this foundation isn't solidified with the seeds of truth and acceptance, the root cause of negativity or any feelings of lacking will potentially hold you back from forward movement.

Moreover, the second principle of awakening is to recognize the enemy from within, that it is of the developmental imagery of your own consciousness. As mentioned, the programming and implementation by the principalities of this world are intended to obstruct your purpose. For instance, you've learned to view yourself in the ways of this world, to dress like others, look like others, and to idolize others in order to prevent you from knowing who you really are.

The world wants you to fit within its boundaries, its limits, and its time constraints—this is done by the implementation of splendor, glamour or any form of idealistic sensationalism that would cause you to doubt who you were created to be—these are why most are distracted from their happiness, wealth, and prosperity.

Within these pages will ignite the path back toward your goal-driven achievements, confidences and riches just to name a quick few. Always remember when you focus on your desired success, the responsibility of maintaining your purpose remains. Wealth is only a small part of who you are; you can be filthy rich and overflowing with currency but still lack the freedoms of love, security, and happiness. This is why it's imperative to find yourself first; it is in knowing your true self that you can yield the power of your love, relationships, and wealth. Perhaps you've heard the old African proverb "If there's no enemy from within, the enemy outside can do us no harm." It is with this understanding that the battle is already won: the acceptance. Furthermore, the next step is submitting to the impeccable valor of truth, placed in your spirit far before your body came into existence.

When you submissively accept your limitations, your faults, and true character, no words, corrupted perceptions or manipulation from the outside world can uproot the solidified integrity of your mental structure. You are now as you were created to be: one within the unfathomable wisdom of the Holy Spirit, immeasurable and without boundaries. It is in this form that the battles will be won. Rejoice in the acceptance of the truth, because now comes the hard part. More specifically, now begins your turning away from your embedded perceptions of the world, closing your eyes against the reflection in the mirror, and then journeying through the darkness of your mind to find the illumination waiting to be revealed.

Chapter 8
Journey through the Darkness

This darkness of which I speak of isn't the darkness of fear but the darkness of purposeful wonders shrouded within the confusions, denials, and misconceptions of your consciousness. Consider these areas of dark, vast channels, blocks, and barriers as a labyrinth of sealed fate, created to protect what's deeply embedded within your mental storehouse. You've known the path since conception, and only you possess the keys to the uncharted paths stored and locked away for your journey's sake. This manifested darkness of protection will nurture you through if you will it to be; in this you will be led to the light of your true self: limitless, selfless, and without form. It is in this place that you will acquire the knowledge of peace as you pass through, which in turn will manifest the power to mold your world, mind, and body. Recall that consequences are also present if you choose to deviate from your intended path, lest you lose your way. For instance, a flower was created to bloom; it has the grand purpose of pollination, aroma, and beauty. It bears life-giving nutrients for the unaltered purpose of being as one within the circle of life. At any given time if it's uprooted from its nutrient-base environment, it will no longer be able to sustain or fulfill the covenant of its existence. Notice the recurring plant examples? (hint). This is to the heart of my purpose; even as a child I understood that I was to share the analogies of life as they were impressed upon my soul within the Comforter.

Know that my thoughts are but a reflection of the source that healed my broken soul. Now enlightened, I understand I am a part of you, as we are travelers and seekers of the light within the unfathomable realm of the subconscious. It is such a privilege to know we all share in this covenant of life, as well as its wonders of peace and fulfillment. In truly understanding this, I gain not only solitude when I'm dealing with others, but also the ability to embrace life, happiness, as well as an abundantly filled heart. Since the perception of our time began, laws and boundaries have governed certain physics, dimensions, and consciousness. Laws of polarity, manifestation, and vibrations are amongst these, but they wouldn't exist without acknowledging their intended purpose. For example, the law of gravity exists because the balance of life was created to sustain humanity.

In other words, as mentioned prior, would life on earth exist without the properties and gravitational pull of the sun or moon? Would the waters remain in place or choose not to yield to the masses of land for the perfection of earth's balance? We laugh, we cry, we breathe in then exhale out. Ultimately we live and then we pass on, further obeying the law of polarity according to the realm were currently flowing through. This is a universal law, yet we turn from the truth that we are universal beings, simply existing in what we've come to believe is our own personal time or our own significantly little-personal space. We are as one within the unfathomable wisdom of the spirit, yet most often feel alone and disconnected.

These are but some of many comparisons to the meaning of life, a balance that we all desire to be a part of, but again often find ourselves farthest from the epiphany of enlightenment.

Even though we've firmly planted the seeds of purpose within the soil, we somehow get distracted by the lurking darkness of our paths. As mentioned, the darkness of which I speak of isn't fear, but purposeful wonder. Our minds are protected with a barrier, shrouded within itself as the darkness between consciousness and the subconscious. This barrier acts similar to the nutrient-dense soil I spoke of earlier when I referenced a flower that was created to bloom. As such, our minds will bloom upon the acknowledgment of truth, saturation of purpose, and commitment to ascend to a higher consciousness. Upon this, the awakening will come, bringing forth the seeds of your greatness, positive manifestations and answers to your purpose filled blessings.

Again, the acknowledgment of the power we all have dwells within our subconscious. As for myself, I've been enlightened to call upon its name as the Comforter, the Holy Ghost, or the Holy Spirit. Some see this entity as the subconscious mind, a supernatural being, or the universe—but no matter what you call this wonder, it's limitless, it's alive, and it is and has always been a part of you. The only issue is that all we've gotten to know from our very first breath is the temporary vessels we reside in; of course I'm talking about our bodies. Magnificently and wonderfully made within the secrets of our mother's womb, these miracles of light are but another example of the powers between the realms of reality. No man can comprehend the covenant of this bond.

When speaking on God's covenant, I digress from speaking on any other subject matter, being as the bond between God and woman is infinitely sealed. This is why not only do I consider woman the closest being to God, but also I chose to write about their bond in another book, again to show honor to all that is woman.

The subconsciousness within our minds is like the fertile soil of the earth; it only knows the power of growth, infinite in its wisdom as the positive flow of massive energy. Like any seed or suggestion planted deep within the darkness of the soil, the seed will manifest its intended properties. In short, if you plant the seeds of flowers, your plot will flourish in beauty; conversely, if you plant that which is not meant to flourish, you will reap no harvest and only turmoil will rise. This is known, said many different ways over the course of our history; beginning with "you'll reap what you so."

Know that the subconsciousness within your mind is like a vast garden, and your thoughts are the goals, ideas, or dreams you desire to manifest. The only concern is that your subconsciousness will do its job of fertilization whether the goals, ideas, or dreams are to your advantage or not. This is why it's absolutely imperative to govern your thoughts with positive affirmations and faith in goodness and the abundance of life. In doing this, you will reap the abundance and wealth of your greatest faith, hopes, and prayers.

Here's a little something I picked up from the battlefield on my way back many journeys ago; I call it "the difference in wealth."

I spoke with a figure who was ill-prepared for the journey; he stated that with all of his power, influence, and money, he had never felt loved. He went on to ask, "Do you know what the difference is between a poor man and a rich man?" To me it appeared to be a no-brainer—that is until he said, "None. There is no difference, being as both are driven by fear." He said he had walked the earth for 234 years, until the day of his passing, and all that he had thought was glory turned out to be a fading memory. "Both men are fools," he said, "with one in fear of losing it all, and the other in fear of losing all that he has."

I gathered the understanding that each man was so selfishly desperate to achieve his embedded desires that he failed to give out of his true purpose. We all have a path and purpose to follow, that yearning drive to be established or the insatiable desire in which to solidify immortality. Unfortunately, this journey is filled with delusions, and at times we drift in the face of uncertainty. Having fallen into deceived consciousness, we find ourselves treading in a sea of despondency.

As confusing as this stage is in our lives, to escape, we only need to realize that we've become intoxicated with the negative principalities of this world, in doing so, we've mistakenly stumbled off the natural course of life.

We are easily distracted from the truth as we visualize the world revolving around us, first ignoring the law of attraction set in place, which are perfectly calibrated to sustain the covenant of life, and then by barreling ignorantly forward to solidify the spirit driven by dismay. All forms of life as we know it obey the natural truth as a whole, not as individual species but as a single essence in purpose.

Furthermore, other forms of life blend into the very fabric of existence as well, without questioning the integrity or instinctual purpose of their nature. Each creature that is created dwells within its laws to sustain its evolutionary path and, in doing so, takes part in the mortality of its existence. For example, the balance of the ocean and the life within it transitions peacefully in its purpose; the understanding water gives breath within itself in the perpetual foundation of its ecosystem.

Even the fowl of the air recognizes the limits and balances amongst the land, sea, and atmosphere. It's fully aware it can only soar so high or nest comfortably below, and anything else would serve no purpose for its existence. And what of the land itself—does it not follow the embedded law of attraction in order to sustain itself and prosper? Does the mighty tree not withstand the winter yet provide shelter; does it not absorb the sunlight to enrich the planet with oxygen and produce life-giving fruit for the nourishment of all?

Only humans question the purpose of life, though having the same power within nature to produce and maintain the covenant bestowed upon them.

Often we choose to dwell upon our own misconstrued purposes and self-induced fallacies about living, but is that actually life? If, walking through a majestic garden, you noticed a plant not producing fruit, a sweet aroma, or vibrant color even though its environment was favorable, you would conclude that the plant was dead and proceed to uproot it, with the earnest intention of preventing its decay from infecting the beauty of its surroundings.

I've mentioned this in earlier chapters but know It's needed to speak aloud, again and again as to continuously acknowledge the truth into our existence. In other words repeating awareness affirmations until it manifests into understanding.So in comparison, what then of humans not producing fruit nor prospering in favorable conditions—is carrying out the anatomical function of breathing enough to consider a human living or simply a human being? The very definition of *being* means existence, so when we correlate human beings with existence, life is their self-fulfilling purpose. Living a life for the fulfillment of God's covenant is the purpose in its entirety, and embedded within his purpose lies the blueprint of life, giving rise to the peace of attraction. Encompassing this understanding will allow you to bear witness to the truth and the answer of our existence.

If you have breath, give breath; if you've acquired wisdom, teach wisdom; if you are nourished, then give nourishment; and if you have life, then reproduce. Give unto others as you'd want people to give unto you, as the Holy Bible says.

That's why the mountain remains still and the tree is so deeply rooted. We all have a purpose, but until we accept that purpose, our vision becomes a blur and our minds become foggy, easily confused to the point of apathy. At this stage, life becomes a question rather than a purpose, and the absence of purpose births doubt without reason, creating the fear of being forgotten.

So, woefully confused, we that is the consciousness of man, rushes through life gathering a quantity of things, titles, and riches to bolster our self-esteem, all the while using massive amounts of time and energy just digging ourselves deeper into unfertilized soil. When we fear purpose, we manifest an abyss within the mind; for this reason we may find ourselves asking the rhetorical question again and again: "What's the purpose of life?"

Just know that when you've accepted the diligent path of obedience, your seeds will have broken through the darkness of the soil, transforming from their hardened shells into the maturity of their intended purposes. Now you can yield your harvest unselfishly and allow it to flourish within the light of this world.

In doing this we join others as we usher in the enlightened ways of a higher consciousness.

Chapter 9
The Light of the World

This journey within will lead you to a place of pure exhaustion—know that this is an absolute necessity, being as it is where you should be in the transparency of the moment. It is in this state that your mind will submit to the humility needed to finally hear and absorb the little voice that has been whispering in your spirit since birth.

Welcome to who you were created to be; now it's time to get to work. First, let's start by asking, "Who are you?" I can't answer this question for you, but know that you're standing at the threshold of your mental storehouse and you have waiting at your discretion the keys to all the skill sets, clairvoyant insights, and talents given—the very gifts you've unknowingly fallen upon as the foundation throughout the struggles of your life, including relationships, goals, and accomplishments. Any wrong choices, bad decisions, or persuasions you've fallen victim to in the past are no longer of concern; the purpose remains intact and ready for you to continue your walk.

Understand and believe you've accomplished exactly what the purpose of life requires, that is maintaining breath within your temple; thanks to the subconscious. This immeasurable life-giving property holds the key to transmitting spirit into existence with regard to your functionality in this world.

Now is the time to awaken with zoey life and step out in faith with any decision on your heart, you are now connected with a source you may have never called upon. For in this found treasure chest of gifts exists an audible connection to your heart; remember this requires absolute faith, so ignore any voices of doubt. Humbly listen and follow the heartfelt energy field, as this will clear any blocks previously holding you back from success, financial prosperity, and happiness. Allow your newfound confidence to destroy the strongholds and deceptive barriers that have rooted themselves in your subconscious.

You are untouchable. No pain or confusion can halt your direction. Now is the second for commitment. Grasp this moment and take your marriage back with unconditional valor, don your battle gear, and take control of your home; for this is where you make your stand. First, take back your mind from any previous failures or feelings of guilt which drained your inner peace. Gather yourself now and reconstruct your home. Let forgiveness cleanse your house and cultivate wisdom in every corner. Do this by speaking positive affirmations and faith based ideas as you walk through preparing for a new harvest within your sanctuary.

Share this aloud, and it will echo positive focus in the hidden crevices where negativity used to wait. It is here where your secondary battle begins, your house is your home; which is the battlefield of the physical realm. Immediately throw out any seeds of manipulation that could manifest the negative yields of past vices; in this you'd disregard the cunnings of old temptations.

Cast away all forms of that which could sabotage your true purpose: alcohol, pornography, any form of nicotine or drugs that pull your temple to idle self-pleasures, this includes fears, lust of any kind, and doubt. This should be done in order to complete the next battle.

This next task resides in the person you've abused outwardly, while your mind was shrouded in darkness; this battle resides in the product of your relationship. Take ownership first, submit your issues, and ask for forgiveness for any destruction your uncharted path could have caused within your relationship.

Now, just as you did within your mind, you need to listen, allow your heart to open, and prove that you'll do whatever it takes to make right your world and the people affected within it. Look into their spirits and allow your enlightenment to become infectious with love; take partnership with a newfound purpose. Complete conviction during this secondary battle taking place in your home will strengthen your journey as you travel—now take hold of the acquired knowledge and proceed forward. The specifics of how to do battle with the vices in your life will be covered another time, but for now know that doubt is nonexistent; you have what is required for victory. Say this again, out loud repetitively so as to saturate the walls of your sanctuary and speak it into existence. Allow the reconstruction of your thought process to unfold abundance in the reality of your uncluttered perceptions. Remember, most dwell on depressive things as to become depressed. If you fixate on a subject, you'll become the subject.

This is also true with the positive suggestions and affirmations I'm asking you to speak loudly in your home, especially so others can hear the winds of blessed change coming their way. No longer do you need anything outside of your environment, cleansing starts from within. Anything else could otherwise weaken your stance causing you to fail. Speak these words "Doubt is nonexistent; I have what is required for victory," bring this into existence immediately! Say it over and over again with absolute and total confidence in order to pave the way back to your intended path.

Know that there is acknowledgment within this journey. Seemingly miracles of connections and positive coincidences will appear all around, but remember that true sight needs to be acquired before abundance can be drawn close; in other words, your clarity will see through any distractions. All our lives we've search for inspiration, from our parents, friends and teachers, but understand that inspiration will only last within the company of itself. The moment you walk away from the inspiring one, the task of holding that flame is solely yours, but that which isn't acquired by commitment will most assuredly fade away.

Then there's the chase of motivation—nothing gets the momentum up faster than the push of motivation, but as with inspiration, the push of motivation will eventually lose traction and you'll find yourself farther from where you began.

Now alone, you find yourself coming down from an emotional high but without the strength or true understanding of how you got there, not to mention what you will need to get you through your circumstances.

Again I say, what you need is what has been with you all along, buried deep within but readily available for your awakening. By now you should be asking yourself, "What is it? That is, if you can put yourself in a momentary state of mindfulness. Whereas you're not being distracted by politics, purposeful attempt by trouble makers or the perceived stressors within and around our environment. What's in me that has always been a part of me? What are these gifts that's been spoken of?" As I said before, we will confirm each other in truth, and it is in this spirit where we all share certain powers, but for now I'm speaking of the word commitment. This is a self-driven powerhouse that will supersede anyone's words of inspirations, anyone's persuasive motivations, and even the darkness of your own self-inflicted fears, worries, or failures.

Know that when you take a stand, an oath, or a covenant, you invoke one of your greatest assets, camouflaged deeply within the depth of your heart. When you were a child, they called it stubbornness or foolish pride, but now the seed has emerged mature, so we call it commitment according to its intended purposes.

I too was stubborn as a child and often whimsically foolish like so many others at that age. Only in my case, something happened, while playfully fighting the spiritual battles to be.

Something quite unexpected that existed far before a time, thought once my own; soon to be revealed as truth while in its bosom. In this acknowledgment, it will catapult you through your struggles; again I say "commitment!"

It is yours to wield, belonging to you, manifesting as it awaits your faith to be fully tested. This power needs no reason for its purpose, other than forward movement; its path serves no other master, intention, or outward persuasions. Just like the garden produces to fulfill its purpose, commitment will produce whatever you manifest either by faith or by default; the result will be by your own hands.

Remember the harvest of your commitment is in direct proportion to your intended goal, which in turn brings your purpose into reality. You may not feel this power at the moment, but it resides in you nonetheless. You may even question its strength because of failed attempts in the past or failures in any other areas of your life. I impress upon you that apathy isn't your intended path; you were meant to be a light of shining authority and respect, not an excuse for low moral or hidden character. Look deeply; remember you were created to bloom, resilient in strength, empowered with wisdom, and blessed with the endurance to weather the storm. Recall that a delicate flower wasn't created to flourish in the desert, but it will flourish greatly in the lush environment that it was intended to grow.

This is who you are. It represents your life, your relationships, your true character, and even your spiritual journey.

If the environment isn't conducive to the very nature that dwells within, you will become hardened, bitter, and dissatisfied.

If this takes place, your very aura itself will spread out and destroy any positive flow within your reality, including goals, careers, or finances. This is not for you—destruction is not your path. Any barriers or entrapments that bring about any form of hurt, either by you or an outside influence, can be rectified. This can be effortlessly done by no longer allowing past issues, guilt, or insecurities or even unexplained circumstances to hinder the power of happiness meant for you. Utilizing the strength of faith to overcome while acquiring the courage to rise above all that would try to condemn your purpose is completely within your reach.

Accept that there is life in and all around you, waiting to be taken control of by the presence of your will. Just know that if you choose the illusion of pride to force this or any other selfishly driven goal, you will only advance where you began, never truly breaking any barriers within your environment. For instance, your consciousness can create an image of what you believe your desires to be. Only remember: the enemy dwells within your weighted consciousness, and due to the constant bombardment of implanted insecurities, injustices, and self-induced fears, the unconquered mind isn't to be relied upon. This is why you must battle through the barriers of manifestations, miseducation, and the darkness within the mind—doing this enlightens the path toward your mental treasures.

Until certain barriers of your thought process are conquered, forward movement will cease to exist, fading away into the abyss of your subconscious. You have the power, you possess the strength, and only you can complete this journey.

If you choose otherwise, by not accepting your purpose or task you fail by default; furthermore, you will still be waiting to be awakened. Why do this? It takes the same amount of energy to have faith as it does to create fear! Know that if you concentrate on the positive as much as you dwelled on the negative, you'll find out that molding reality isn't as difficult as you once thought. Please do not allow forces from within to persuade you into complacency; understand that there are no grounds for false contentment. If you submit to this clouded vision, you will continually question yourself and hold yourself in a perceived form of contentment, encompassing an unfulfilling life of discouragement.

This is a burden that not only steals your life-force but in turn hinders anyone within your surroundings, especially the people that look up to you in faith that you're doing something great in life; remember that you're their hope as well. As I mentioned, you were meant to be a light, a source of strength and acknowledgment, so letting yourself down will cause a loss of energy within all that's around you.

Even though the power to overcome still resides within every breath you take, every missed opportunity to course correct your life, your abilities, or your purpose will cause them to fade even deeper into the darkness.

Please recall that the light of your leadership is needed, and your presence must yield its enlightenment for no other path was meant for you. Become who you were created to be in this world, let your commitment ignite your spirit with confidence and joy, and remember we are "as one." My trust is within you; draw upon it as needed. My faith is in your heart; let it whisper confidence during the lonely or trying times.

My spiritual commitment is to love you and see you through as we are connected through the words of this book. My heartfield is resonating outwardly into every page touched by the warmth of your hand. As memories created within the transparency of your fingerprints, swiping across the letters of both our commitment in reading this book; we've become one with each page turned. Rest on this as foundation in the spirit, until you're strong enough to return this moment of connection within the needs of humanity, forevermore.

Chapter 10
The Transparency of a Novice

By now we've witnessed the language, confirmed the testimonies, and heard the truth, but even still the process remains difficult. Why is this? It's because knowing the truth is only the first step in taking a path to a successful way of life. We must continue to combat the everyday attacks that weaken our journey. Being as we're wrapped up in the flesh of our temples, it's easy to fall off course. Just remember the war has already been won, and falling or failing aren't the end; neither does this mean *you* are a failure; it simply mean temptations of the flesh are always waiting for the opportunity to try and distract you again and again.

Understand, how you look at the difficulties of the world can create devastating impacts throughout your life. Why? Because, as mentioned in previous chapters, your subconscious remains endowed with powers and resources beyond your greatest wonders, but only if you choose to call them forth in your life. The subconscious doesn't care what you plant or command it to do; its job is to produce, and produce it will, always and forevermore. As it was spoken, the law of polarity dictates a balance between the pull and lack thereof within a person's journey.

What this means 100 percent of the time is, when you're going through the tribulations of life, you're constantly finding yourself battling the principalities and strongholds of this world; laid waste in your mind. Know that the forces of good are being cultivated and produced to the equivalent degree within your mental storehouse. Your subconscious is ready to birth the seeds of influence, favor, and regeneration. Just as all exist in the balance of nature and reality, so does your life on earth. If you choose to have a piece of heaven while walking your path, it's more than possible for it has already been done! I've written a few testimonies, dreams, and examples from my own experiences, but I kept it light because I want you to focus on the many analogies the Holy Spirit has given me throughout my life. If the analogies appear difficult to comprehend or even believe, know that's quite acceptable.

For instance, I could make a sandwich and explain in detail how delicious it looks, but the level of my personal experience with the savory taste of the sandwich can only go so far, being as the experience requires other senses to validate the message I'm trying to relay.

Here's the really nice thing: I've been a professional chef for over twenty years, and with my experience in visual appeal, aroma, and taste, I can transcend the senses by giving you detailed information on how to construct such a sandwich. This way you can experience the taste for yourself, but only if you commit to following the exact recipe created out of my culinary knowledge. The recipe for the sandwich draws upon my experiences and knowledge as a professional chef.

So when you really think about it, there's no difference between my giving you directions for making a sandwich and my sharing the path I took for awakening consciousness with the analogies given to me over time by way of the Holy Spirit. These were my experiences, and I've diligently utilized the knowledge from each trial, vision, and passing to transcend my state of mind; in this I found great power. I know that it's a part of my purpose to open up and share what I've learned, and I acknowledged many years ago that this was not a burden but a blessed privilege.

Also, I'd like for you to know I've held onto my teachings since childhood, so as to prove my temperament was molded correctly. In other words, I held on to them to prove that what I learned actually works, as opposed to sorting through all the false prophets of misguided purposes scattered within the journey—but know that's not a bad thing. Remember, some people are needed to challenge or agitate you to get up and seek the real truths along your path. Having said this, I'd also like to say I absolutely love when I hear teachers, ministers, and philosophers get it right—but who am I to question the doctorates? I mean, the true origin of their knowledge stemmed from somewhere remember? This is why I acknowledge someone's understanding by way of their walk, not by the judgment of their fall, being as the truth within their power always arises, if ever, after the descent.

As mentioned before, in my travels I've met many obstacles, and I've encountered some powerfully convincing people as well. Yet by way of the spirit that dwells within me, I didn't allow a person's manipulations or words to guide me from my focused path. If the knowledge they gave was conducive to my overall purpose or sacrifice that lead to enlightenment, I'd take note, research, and meditate within the clarity of mind.

In this process, the truth would reveal itself and further give rise to confirmed spiritual results, not just the reliance upon another's inspired words. Remember, inspiration only serves its purpose within the environment of the moment, and that's great for getting an exhausted team pumped up during halftime. However, what we need during our journey is confirmation within the spirit that will invoke our commitment to carry on to fulfill our destiny. While on the subject, let's not forget about being motivated by way of leadership—this is another great tool if wielded with good intent, but recall what happens after it dwindles down, hours later.

As I said before, you may inadvertently find yourself back in the same mental position but in a different environment. This in turn may beat you down spiritually, being as you didn't acquire the knowledge you needed for the leap into your new circumstance. The result is that you're back where you started before you sought out the motivation. Think of a boxer getting beaten badly before returning to his corner in complete disarray. Then the trainer provides great advice and motivates him to step out and do things a different way, and chances are it will help for the time being.

Moreover, what happens when the other opponent changes the battle plan? The slightly less than motivated boxer is left once again, alone in the ring desperately trying to hold on to knowledge he never fully acquired on his on. This is why commitment to a cause is so vitally important. Remember, *for no other reason than to push forward.*

If you're ill-prepared in life or in your thought process, you'll learn more from the trials and errors than you'd ever learn from being motivated to take life on unprepared. I say this to bring up the importance of the steps spoken earlier; know that I gave just enough explanation so that one day you'll see the confirmation, if not already. So if you find yourself bumping your head against a wall, saying, "What is this guy talking about?" just stay committed to the goals saturated within your heart. In other words, please don't allow my inability to reach you with my stories to sway you to close your mind. Stay focused; this is why there are many different speakers of light, and just as you are, I'm still in transition. We all have a higher calling, so reach until you find a concept you can hold onto firmly. What follows next is a foothold to balance upon, and before you know it, you're officially on your path, fully committed in your spirit to guide you to enlightenment.

Your focus is especially important when dealing with people that convince, promise, or persuade you for whatever reason. Understand that commitment needs no pat on the back and no psychologically motivated push; it is what it does by way of its will, and you should trust in it.

This is why, when someone is telling me a story, instead of judging the storyteller before the picture is painted, I simply acknowledge the action produced from the story. Don't trust words behind the fog; the truth revealed can be witnessed by the actions it manifests. This is why I speak transparently; in this you can see my true intentions, which are to give and not take.

Remember, there are demonic influencers with the intent to misdirect you, well prepared to pull out all the quotes, Bible scriptures, and mixed-opinionated confidences, with the intent of leading you off your path. Accomplishing this only brings light to the storyteller, not to the listener, and as soon as you submit your trust, you'll find fault in the leader's actions. This development is just enough distraction to cause you to turn from your path, accomplishing the deceiver's original goal. Remember, some barriers are meant to be agitating to the mind, testing its vulnerability, causing you to seek for yourself. It's my intent to mentally hold hands with you, spiritually confirming that upon beginning this travel, you will find your way through the darkness; it's achievable, whether you choose to believe it now or later—either through my intent in writing or through your own trials, all will come to pass as truth.

As an example, you know that deep within you resides great power, you've felt it all your life, but you've also at some time embodied guilt, depression, or fear obtained from the many distractions otherwise repressed throughout your struggles. Having said this, accept the realization of the many pitfalls along the way—this clarity can point you toward the path of your gut feeling.

You know, that unforeseen pull, your intuition or better yet the origin to that little voice that has positively kept you from falling off the deep ends throughout your life; quiet the chatter and I promise you'll hear it.

Have faith in knowing you're moving toward your purpose, even if you haven't figured it out just yet. The conquered manifestations can be utilized as the footholds necessary to propel you over or through any past repressions. At this point in your life, it's okay to challenge what you've learned over the course of your trials and tribulations. You cannot say the enlightened path doesn't exist, considering all the many examples of good versus evil you encounter from adolescence to adulthood. If you fail to acknowledge all the stories from Prince Charming to the coming of Christ, you might sabotage your walk within the journey.

If this is happening, set aside your guilt, your self-induced worries, and suggested fears. In doing so, you will confirm all that I and others out of the transparency of truth speak upon—not because we are special, but because you are in so many ways. So deny letting the world mold your reality and take control of your life. Again, I'm not trying to convey that I'm masterfully intelligent on the subject of spirituality and consciousness, but rather that I'm a person committed to sharing what I've learned spiritually, physically, and mentally, while enduring the path of life's many issues. The evidence of my triumphant battles against the principalities of this world proves positive by surviving the many life-draining potholes I've fallen into.

And yes, climbed out of despite all whom wanted me to fail, still found the strength to pull myself forward, back onto my path, thanks to the seeds of commitment. Again, I'm not asking that you trust by my words alone but instead by the integrity of my spirit.

If you look deep enough within yourself, you'll find that I and many others speak in truth. Confirmations are all along this journey; you'll come to find them. We're all one within this spiritual battle. We have been endowed with an appropriate amount of greatness, and speaking this in confidence will connect you with others like you and confirm my integrity as well. Until then, read this book over and over again, really pick over the chapters, and you'll find it's divided into certain spirit-filled channels, embedded to help connect you with the greatness residing in your subconscious.

This will happen as you read and eventually as you begin your travels in rest. It's just waiting to be revealed, pulled forth, and utilized to a great degree and as you'll see fit. On the surface, my words may not appear as impactful as the accepted professionals', but I have humbly shared some experiences in trust that you will receive a connection. This is because I've chosen to step out on faith and write, as I was told within the breaking of the seed, "Come as you are! You have something to say!" Boldly this was spoken within my spirit, and I willingly stepped up to the challenge. Without hesitation, I ignored my past issues with dyslexia, miseducation, and fear of persecution since I'm not trained as an author.

I was also told, "Go forth diligently and in truth" and tell my story of imperfection, regardless of my past circumstances, problematic situations, or environmental barriers; being the Holy Spirit will guide my words, oversee my actions and hold firm my walk upon his foundation. So as you see, we are truly one within this journey, both seeking the next step to a higher consciousness and both realizing that we share a common greatness, that is the ability to commune on a conscious level.

It was also revealed that I'll have others of great leadership in writing assist my purpose, when I submit totally to the cause, either by the journey within the realm or by the giving of another experience. Please excuse me if my expressiveness is a bit repetitive, but as stated, I want to be as transparent as possible. In this state, I believe I will get the best of criticisms and acknowledgment of any misconstrued issues or mistakes. Also, if the appearance of my tone is authoritative, know my goal is to only speak within the humbling experiences learned throughout my trials. Whether you're reading this soon after I wrote it or twenty years from now, I'm still humbly in the spirit of our communion.

In fact, I'm receiving your feedback by every letter pronounced or visualized into thought. It's in the same process that we can pray for each other and strengthen our journeys as we continue to climb within the stairs of the enlightened path. Remember, you mostly achieve the consciousness of man by losing who you think you are and embracing the person God created within you. This is possible within the continuous now, being that the now transcends past, present, and future.

For instance these assembled letters form words, and words produce sound, and as mentioned prior, sound is vibrations resonating throughout the air. The air you breathe is the same I breathe, no matter how far apart we are; we reside within the same atmosphere. This breath is of the past, present, and future, no different from the words spoken in this book. So, whether you read this yesterday, today, or tomorrow, upon pronunciation of its words, it's considered the now, transcending time.

Or how about this analogy: where does the Earth start or finish if you're walking a straight line? Some would argue, "It depends on where you start," but others will be perplexed by the notion, wondering, "Is there an actual start where God placed a grain first, and then proceeded to finish the rest of the planet?"

To some this is an oversimplified question, serving no purpose. For others, they can't wrap their minds around it but one day, someone more experienced than I will explain it to them. To keep us on track, understand this question wasn't meant to be answered. It was spoken as an analogy, to help you visualize the immortality of the oxygen we've inhaled within our lungs since before Christ walked the planet. It is difficult to comprehend at times, but think about it like this: Say you've just got married, and you're deeply in love. You say your vows and, without any preparation on your part, you find your spouse is suddenly transported three thousand miles away. Do you think the power of your love would suddenly diminish?

Not at all—it would remain as powerful as if you were standing right next to each other.

Now, imagine that your spouse called and said, "I just got transported three thousand miles away, and I can't come back!" What feeling would you experience? Would you suddenly feel hurt? Why would this be causing you pain? You wouldn't have physically been touched, but the feeling of drastic pain would be powerful enough to bring you to your knees. This represents the energy of feeling between spaces. This feeling is immeasurable, no matter how far the distance is between you and your loved one. This connection resides as a power source within your consciousness.

Women normally have a better understanding of feelings like this, simply because they have a natural intuition or what could be described as an incredible bonding of clairvoyant understanding. This is why women are being continually attacked in mind, body, and spirit more than any other being on the planet—but as mentioned in an earlier chapter, I'm saving that topic to show honor within another book.

As mentioned a few times, I'm no professional, at least not yet—that'll be a discussion and a debut years from now when I'm presenting at a seminar, transformational presentation or world speaking event. Until then, know that this book is just the beginning of what I was created to do. And having said this, I promise to honor the art and embodiment of a great author so as to share my unique vision within the purpose of our journey.

Chapter 11
Travelers Amongst Us

Hello again. In the previous chapter I spoke on my experience, submitting to you that I'm considered a novice as a writer, and that's a totally acceptable criticism, which I deeply appreciate receiving. My actual experience is in surviving the strongholds in life. I've used these experiences to overcome and enjoy the abundances of life in complete happiness! Although I've suffered many trials, failures, and setbacks, I absolutely love life and all the mysteries, experiences, and connections within my reach and those yet to be encountered.

Some would ask, "How can you have abundance and complete happiness, if you've also stated within the same sentence that you 'suffered many trials, failures and setbacks'?" Let me explain: Have you ever heard the phrase "peace on earth"? I'm sure you have and know that within your subconscious is where you truly live and experience life. No matter what your outward circumstances, environmental situation, or physical awareness, no one can truly take your peace.

Even in imprisonment, there are no limitations on your mind; choose peace, choose happiness, and live within your spirit. Stating this again and again changes your reality. Here's a quick bonus as to help bridge your understanding.

Originally I was saving this for my future book, *Analogies Revealed*. But being there are so many stories, I'll share this one to prepare and build that bridge, furthermore showing just how powerful your mind is when it comes to bringing forth a physical change in this reality.

Let's talk about healing: this requires your body to respond in a way that's conducive to repair. Ask yourself, can you heal your body or rid it of disease at will? Yep, absolutely you can if you focus or meditate on it daily. So, here's my point: Ever heard of someone crying at will, possessing the ability to shed tears in order to convince you of their issues? How about creating a mental image of a lust so strong that it causes your body to create goose bumps, sexual arousal, and the feeling of euphoria? Most do this on a daily basis, and that's the point. If you focus or meditate effectively enough, your subconscious will respond, creating a physical change, even if it's to flush out disease within your body. Let's not forget the opposite side of this track. Some people focus so much on the negative, moaning, "Woe is me," or complaining, that they actually bring depression and shrouded circumstances of turmoil into their lives on a continual basis. If they continue focusing into this deception of will, they'll channel it outwardly to all within their surroundings. Have you ever felt dirty or spiritually bankrupt because you spent time with these beings? This goes for liars, cheaters, evildoers, and deadbeats as well.

You will, without doubt fail if you find yourself encompassing their reality by engaging within their field of negativity for an extended amount of time.

I touched on this in a previous chapter when I spoke about your bank account directly reflecting the people you associate with. Think of it: it's pretty rare to have three friends, one who works with you, another who has been out of work for a while now, and a last friend who's wealthy beyond belief; it's possible but highly not likely. This is why I've stated before, depending on how you perceive the world, the ability to change your perception and manage the forms of enlightenment is yours to control. Imagine you're snowed in on a cold evening in the mountains, nightfall has come, and the stars are full of shimmer.

You grab your favorite book as your loved one snuggles in beside you, embracing with a hug. The lights are dim, the room is rustic, and you're absorbing the warm glow from the fireplace as it gently crackles with sound; at this moment all's right within the world. It doesn't make any difference that it's uncomfortably cold outside, because you've found peace within the structure of your environment. Living in that moment of the now is one of the many powers you have at your discretion, finding the strength in this moment, for peace can be found in all who truly desire peace.

In doing this, perceptions change; either a couple can enjoy each other in the presence of each other's happiness or they can invoke stress about the coldness of the weather—the choice is within their ability of accepted perception. And getting back to criticism, I appreciate all that comes with stepping out on faith, especially the insights or criticisms of my faults, including opinions, views, and interpretations.

All are welcome when the speaker has the best intentions of seeking truth in common ground. It's important to me that you understand that I praise God for your choosing to absorb the transparency of my gratitude and enlightenment.

Know there is room for everyone's purpose to connect with the many ways of finding the abundance in life, even if it leads to the debate of new or misconstrued understandings. I've spoken about my ventures, rendering the availability for scrutiny, judgement and criticisms, now I humbly ask — what about you? Are people criticizing you for stepping out and trying to be what's really tugging at your heart? Are you criticizing yourself with all the negative bombardment that the consciousness of your mind has absorbed over the entirety of your life? If people are in fact criticizing your every move, change the way you perceive their criticisms. Look at it like this: they acknowledge that you exist. This tells you that either something's not lining up with your actions or they have a problem within their own personal interests. Don't waste time trying to prove them wrong; instead, show empathy and stay focused on your journey, after all— life is most often about trial and error; stay the course.

Remember, some entities are really distractions from the true intentions of your positive authority within this world. After recalibrating your mindset, start the process again by way of dealing with any lingering manifestations planted by the distraction—I'm talking deep down within the core of all your secrets, all the fears and insecurities. In this you'll start your battle, in and outside of your reality, bringing forth encouragements along the way.

I could express more of my dreams and analogies, as the spirit has shared with me, but I feel it's time to share just how close you and I could be within this physical realm.

By speaking on the battles within this reality, I wouldn't be surprised to find out just how much we have in common, thanks to the many trials the world had to offer when we were in our vulnerable states; prior to starting our journey. Up until now, people who have known me wonder how I made it through the many barriers I encountered, how I could have been trapped and beaten down by circumstances and still come out free of any wounds and remaining enlightened with joy. I've based my knowledge from the wisdom shared within my soul through spiritual enlightenment, but as I said before, judge not by a person's words or intentions but by their actions. In other words, ask where the proof of my knowledge is; how can you tell if I'm sharing the truth or just trying to capture what others have attempted to witness by way of inspirational speeches, motivational rallies, and those how-to catchphrases.

I'll go into a brief description of my overcoming barriers and breaking through strongholds a bit later, but for now I want to keep the focus on acknowledging the true character of a person's actions, as opposed to the implemented image of success. When someone shares their experiences as I've shared with you, especially for the purposes of self-guidance and clarity of the consciousness, expect some form of spiritual confirmation. I mean really—be on the lookout for something positive that will assist your growth.

No matter what circumstance or position you hold, positive or not, these examples will not only reconnect you with your natural and spiritual persona but will also course correct any areas of your path needed to be spiritually enhanced. There must be some form of confirmation or evidence-based facts when a person is trying to lead by example.

Know that evidence of self-guidance is all around us, often mistaken as the everyday norm, but I've seen men and women emerge as I and some even stronger, breaking through what was thought to consume them, yet triumphing over the odds of the misguided.

I will speak the names of these few; these spiritual warriors prevailing over the wiles and traps of the world perceived. These few I proudly call as friends, emerging and embracing their character as leaders above and beyond. In acknowledging them, I'll speak honor in the name of a brother named Donald, a Royal family by the name of Ellis, Lauren and Chris Fritz, a mother by the name of Linda, a long lost but found family member by the name of Emmanuel Mooty, a family friend by the name of Connie Sears, a chef by the name of Anthony T. Head, a coworker name Charles Henderson, an incredible mother in-law named Sharon Wartinger, a sister by the name of Elthia, a Master barista by the name of Tim Stiffler- Dean, a mentor named Rufus, called to heaven much to soon, as well as a father named Don. Lastly, not to forget a friend whom I've yet to meet in this physical realm.

With this being said, obviously I'm not the only one that has gone through, so for the many people that inspired me by either listening, speaking or even slamming a door in my face, I just want to say thank you.

Furthermore, I've shared with you some influential stories and analogies, which has paved the direction of my life but I've only shared just a few "one-two or even three steps for reaching your fullest potential" type of information.

The reason for this is because everyone's different in their approach to advancing their lives, so what I've tried to do was give you a few key steps for starting your own journey; the "one-two's and how to do steps" are coming later but trust, it'll be right on time. So, here's a short recap. Change your perceptions and how you view the world first and foremost. This means all within your environment that causes you to become distracted or stressed. This includes family members, loved ones, friends, coworkers, social media, vices and even those whom you believe are your enemies. After making peace, speaking forgiveness, and disregarding any forms of negative outside bombardment, it's time to rest. Not fall asleep from pure exhaustion but actually rest, with the intention of healing.

Next, prepare to battle your greatest enemy, the enemy within your mind. This was without doubt my most difficult battle, but I had already been tempered by nearly insurmountable trials of pains, failures, and sacrifices throughout my life, so forward I'd push on. I've learned that you can benefit from my way of spiritual thought if you trust in the process.

I'm sure you've heard of what I'm about to say, but remember it's for the greater purposes of life, and it's the last step of the sequence in which you will find your path.

Unfortunately for some, from what I've experienced, all forms of spiritual elevation require that we suffer or sacrifice something as "an offering," so to speak, toward our mental state. It's no different from being in the gym, lifting weights or hitting the treadmill to gain muscle and lose weight. Please accept that the body needs to be challenged in some form of fast, prayer, meditation, or rigorous focus. No worries if that's not for you; like I said, there are other ways.

I know you're familiar with the likes of going to a religious Bible-based institution, but as it stands this could be a barrier not broken yet in many people's paths. Just know that without true spiritual guidance, you can only go so far before encountering far more powerful spirits not wanting you to pass. I spoke about such a time in my encounters within a dream, being invited to "a game of the fates," which I don't care to mention again so soon.

However, I've got a ringer up my sleeve—here's what I've learned within the spirit: say all the examples of fasting, meditation, or sacrifices the body requires for entering into the spirit realm aren't your thing; it turns out we all experience small fragments throughout our everyday activities that can accumulate to give possible access to the subconscious. These require you to forgive someone who's a thorn in your side at home, work, or play or even in your memory.

Forgiveness is detrimental to conquering the negative forces; upon adding this attribute of forgiveness, you'll expedite your path to enlightenment. With this you will gain access, positively influencing the battle within the mind upon your rest.

More specifically, when you encompass hate, guilt, envy, or unforgiveness in your soul, these negative attributes slow your travel greatly when you channel above or through the many tunnels of the darkness. In other words the burden of your consciousness will weigh you down in place where constant movement is required to pass through.

Remember, this darkness serves a great purpose by trapping many forms of not so great entities that try to catch a ride between realms. But if you're carrying the weight of the unresolved, it will slow your travel enough where you can get caught in the pull of fear and other implanted forms of clutter.

Mending bonds, helping others, and clarifying misconstrued intents or conversations will help greatly by changing your thought process to that of positivity. Simply letting go of the guilt process and the like thereof will prove to be an essential weapon when you reach the battles. In other words, be consciously free of any barriers when they try to take hold of your day, so when you lay down to relax, start with controlled deep breaths and expect the journey to begin.

Upon this, other gifts and confirmations will seem to appear out of nowhere, being as you're officially on the enlighten path.

Don't stress when you get to this stage, because by now you may have uncovered a gift or two from your mental storehouse. These will be a great tool to intervene on your behalf when forces start to attack your focus.

If attacks come sooner than expected, consider yourself truly blessed, but if you fall; just brush off and start the process over again. I can't stress this enough: it's worth it to push forward, as this journey will require you to absolutely change your mindset. This means you'll have to do battle with that abused-since-childhood, overstimulated, continually bombarded by society's consciousness and strongholds. This battle is a must; it's tremendously important if you want to see obstacles moved effortlessly from your path. At this point in the book, as it correlates to your current position in life, if your conscious is saying "But I'm a good person . . ."disregard this thought process. Please understand to give in, is to give up by default. By doing this you're simply brushing off the fear of uncharted self accomplishment.

Conquering the fear of the unknown, for the betterment of finding who you truly are, is a welcomed sacrifice of self. To kneel upon your path, removing even the smallest stone or barrier by casting it away from your journey enlightens your walk. This includes even the subtleness of obstacles as in submitting to that little negative voice mention previously, resulting in default. Just remember: expect to receive what you give out, so please house no negative emotions lest you receive undesired returns.

I've hinted about confirmation, evidence-based facts, proof, and shared experience while seeking information for spiritual growth. In my approach to assisting with your journey, I've based my path and techniques on my experiences, and as for confirmations, I'm confident they will arise when you least expect them yet need them the most.

So that qualifies as evidence-based truths and shared experience within my life's trials. These can be difficult, being as I'm talking about visitations within other realms, dreams, and higher consciousness—so how is truth measured in these expressions? The answer isn't that difficult to comprehend; in fact, it's much easier to witness the proof and evidence of a person's words, again, by simply looking at his or her surroundings.

Not only must a person look the part of enlightenment, but also other forces should go forth and move in ways not understood by conventional methods, such as casting off positive vibrations of love and trust or having unbiased clarity and answers for others to the point of clairvoyance. This is the type of person who, for some reason, always looks toward the good in situations as well as acknowledge the best in others. Since I'm not able to shake your hand at this moment, It would be difficult to feel the truth within my presence, so I'll move on to discussing my surroundings.

The evidence-based facts in my life, which I continuously praise God for, include the fact that I'm standing today, thinking and putting forth positive efforts.

As mentioned, on multiple occasions, I've survived many obstacles without being consumed or bitter, I really love life, and I'm truly happy to be participating in this purpose. Again, try not to judge the storyteller, lest you miss the story, but do acknowledge the actions produced from words spoken. A person's life should be indicative of blessings and truth flowing around them at all time, so instead of looking at expensive clothes, cars, and material things, see if you can feel the true applications of life.

Here's something I came into understanding, upon breaking the mental barriers into enlightenment, I love being in love! That is to say, all that I put effort in should be that special something which tugs at the heart of my passions. I love being an honest husband, a father and a grandfather. I love my jobs, I love my wife and our marriage, I love my many talents of cooking, playing music and writing. I love speaking and helping people, I love my purposes and many responsibilities in life. I love that I was created for the battle and I love God's plans upon my journey. In short and again, I love being in love. With this said, what are you in love with? Are you allowing time to idly pass by hoping that something will spark your interest? We were made to love, we were created to share and express love as we love each other. Anything else is an abomination of purpose; anything else is a precious waste of time.

Remember, what you put in or seed, the garden that is your mind, will reap in harvest. I sow the love of being in love, therefore I harvest my garden, with absolute faith in the return of an overly abundance of love for all.

This is to the heart of my being, transparent and boldly confessed. Judge not for judging is based on opinionated ideology, this is why I say acknowledge a person's actions to get an unbiased and absolute picture of one's true character. Ask yourself, "Does the people you put your trust in walk a righteous path or even a purposed filled path for that matter? Or are they simply comfortable to be around, triggering the default mode of life. It's your choice to allow, just beware it doesn't become your norm?" You'll find out soon enough, being it'll show up not only in life's achievements but in spiritual awareness.

Whatever the outcome is, it'll become apparent in all the actions of a person, including life choices, finances, family developing and legacy leaving. Notice, all within the environment of the person who claims enlightenment; in such you should witness and feel growth, easy vibrational awareness, and refreshed blessed outlooks, completely free of scandal or clutter; in other words you should and feel see peace.

Well, again, what about me? As for now, my proofs are like the many secrets, answers, and hidden spiritual powers embedded within your hands as you read this book. The proof of my intentions is shared through my ability to be vulnerable and open to the challenge of scrutiny; remember the truth will stand for eternity. This is why it's fine for me to share my deepest secrets, memories, and pains, being as you'll see confirmation that we're not all that different. Consider it a calling card that reads, "Here I am, and these are the issues I've overcome and triumphs I've acquired!" In this I truly praise God for how the many circumstances molded me into the survivor that I've become.

I'm a living testimony that gifts are bestowed for many reasons and upon many different people. For instance, while in the bosom of the Holy Spirit, I was shown that one of my gifts was healing after the battle to strengthen others, and I greatly expect that is amongst your powers as well. At first this didn't seem impressive one bit, but the significance came in the form of deeply embedded seeds, bursting forth at a time of desperate need during my struggles in life.

I was endowed with the power not only to do battle against the strongholds of this world, but also to quickly heal from the wounds inflicted by the evildoers cloaked as sheep. After a while it occurred to me that many of us share the same power, but some fall by the wayside when they don't see their opposition through.

This happens when we stop seeking and allow our thoughts to be controlled by the false perceptions within our surroundings. I know that when hearing about the powers from deep within, most want to get to the flashy products sold in the form of "the powers of riches beyond your wildest dreams!" Trust me when I say that, what resides beyond your wildest dreams were placed there for a reason. If you find yourself mingling with what's not a part of your original purpose, the result could be you not fully coming back from the realm of lust and wonders.

This is why your spiritual armor must be intact for the journey; believe me, I know this firsthand.

Understand that maybe you weren't created to be rich, for example; maybe you were created to be a supporter of rich children, family, or friends, helping them to do right when it comes to their influence over this world. My point is, if you rigorously fight and struggle to become who you think you were created to be, chances are you'll never get there, you'll in fact get somewhere but you'll be ill-equipped to remain in the atmosphere; fooled into complacency.

Why? Because if you can't progress through reaching clarity, your thought process remains cluttered with misguided persuasions. Understand: all the gold in the world doesn't matter whatsoever if the holder hasn't transitioned into their true purpose. We've heard this time and time again throughout our lives: "Having all the money in the world is nothing if you don't have love or the honor within yourself to give it away." Most would assume that money is all they need, but when you really look at it, it's not only an obligation but also it reflects on who you truly are in spirit.

People often flash money and expensive things to convince others of their power, supposedly bringing about admiration, but the truth is that money often proves just how insecure they really are, often promoting careless and unresolved characteristics. Here's an example from my culinary days: one day I had the opportunity to eat Kobe beef flown in from China; at that time it was one of the most expensive steaks sold on the market. When I sat amongst the other chefs, they noticed I cooked my steak medium well, and this sparked outrage. "You eat Kobe beef black and blue!" a chef replied—in other words, rare.

I said, "No, I eat what I like, not what others prefer." Also I stated, "My stomach doesn't care if it's steak or a tuna fish sandwich—its purpose is to provide nutrients to my body, not to appease the etiquette of others." Needless to say, this was an abomination within the culinary field, but my focus was always on hospitality for customers, not the idolization of my culinary skills or the mentality of chefs alike.

In other words, if your conscious isn't one with truth in purpose, then your idea of the power that is money will belong to the demonic strongholds manipulating your mind. Know that all the fine cars, vacations, and expensive goods will do nothing for your true happiness if you lay down alone and hurting at night, not to mention the impact of coveting what you could possibly lose the next day. Is there a balance?

Yes, it's called sacrifice. In this, the unconditional giving to and loving others in need of help, knowledge, and wisdom proves to be a power considered a miracle by definition, all within the faithful sacrifices of your love. Ask yourself, how much air do I need to breathe? How much food do I need to eat before I'm full or how about how much water do I need to consume for optimal functionality of my body. Point is you need just the right amount to stabilize your walk upon the journey of life.

Now ask yourself "How many cars do I need to get from work to home, How many houses do I need to get a good night's rest and of course, just how much money do I really need in life to contribute to my existence as a living breathing human being?

Turns out we only need the certain minimum of any resource to maintain, but I get it; bills, family, taxes, comforts, mistakes and insecurities. We can't escape that right? This is why we seek abundance, in other words the overflowing amount of quantified resources that makes us feel free of insecurities. Only issue is, making sure you have the correct understanding of abundance which is conducive to your life.

I was shared spiritual abundance and awareness of self in many realms which adds to the solidification of my eternal life. In this I'm not limited to the wiles and temptations of this world's many lusts and guilt-driven fears ultimately leading to damnation.

So if you've found abundance that's right for you, share it with the less fortunate; in doing so you will be connected with an unlimited power source; as you give, it will be replenished and returned. Also know that yielding the powers of influence does nothing if you are corrupted in spirit. In other words, you can't trick your subconscious into using powers that are not conducive to your nature or purpose. Many have tried to buy their way by the good works of their deeds, but the true consciousness behind the acts pulled them into the darkness of the chambers.

Recall that within my travels, I referenced meeting a being that was consumed by this trap. He was the one who gave the example of the difference between a poor man and a rich man.

Know that the power to avoid this web of trickery is within you, but after you've moved, over or through the darkness, you still have to travel back, channeling into our current reality. Again, if you are not fully prepared, some of your potential talents could be given to another spirit worthy of their potential.

Have you ever woken up from a dream and had a great, life-changing idea, vision, or purpose, but suddenly it started to fade away with every conscious thought? Well, your next-door neighbor may have received it. Even worse, it could have gone to that person at work you never really cared for. Why? Because anything held within your consciousness will be acted upon. In the case of your life-changing idea going to someone else, it's probably because that person was in your mind and what's in your mind dwells close to the subconscious that connects us all.

This is why praying for others and having faith in one another can help in their journey. Being that thought is a vibrational energy, anything residing in your subconscious can be manifested to grow within the vastness of your expectation.

Don't forget: whatever is in your garden of expectations, even the name of the person you don't want to forgive, can keep us connected, distributing your energy, purpose, and in the case above, your life-changing ideas! Know that it's better to forgive people and release them from your mind, so as to let them journey their own paths. This way, by the time you confront each other, any form of contempt or animosity will be swept away.

We all have this power, and many others not even hidden—but some purposely choose to turn away from these, thinking that with believing comes acknowledgment, which leads to certain responsibilities, then on to rules. It seems many people want to be at the top of the mountain but don't want to endure the physical pain it takes to reach the peak.

Realize that it is the physical work that prepares your legs, giving them the strength to endure the powerful wind blowing over top the mountain. These rules often go against most people's ideas of freedoms, lust, or embellishment, but know that the rules for obtaining enlightenment serve the purpose of freeing your soul and assisting others around you. This provides the examples for breaking through the idealistic bonds of guilt.

It's discouraging how people think into existence, the negative manifestations of fears within their lives. Indulging in this form of fear only brings about the self-fulfilling prophecy of misguided intentions and delusions.

Please know that your abilities to give and attract powers like true love and revitalization will be there when you're ready to submit. Depending on what your true intentions are, you'll be awakened to produce amazing results within your travels, teachings, and leaderships. Any other less than noble intentions will fall within the saying "you'll reap what you sow!"

REGINALD O'NEAL GIBSON

Chapter 12
The Perspective

Time is of the essence within the consciousness of man; it is this thought process that obstructs our spiritual path to enlightenment. In other words, slow down and figure out where your destiny awaits. When the mind loses its way within the darkness, the manifestations of strongholds attack the consciousness, but while on your journey, if you encounter positive heterosuggestion, change is imminent. From this positive influence emerges a great light.

In this faith lies the hidden purpose, deep within the mental storehouse of our subconscious, limitless in its law and readily available for the awakening. We were created for the purposes of life, implanted with greatness and power, not only for survival in this world but for love, happiness, and true abundance throughout the realms into eternity. I wanted to recap the previous statements one more time, as if to speak into existence the honest purposes of our journeys. Wherever we seek knowledge, know that confirmation by the spirit must be manifested positively into our lives. I've opened up a bit on occasion and spoken by way of the Holy Spirit as best I could, sharing my dreams, visions, and analogies. If any of this was a miss, I understand, and that's okay; you'll have your own awakenings soon and hopefully we can reconnect with my next book—in it there will be analogies explained in full detail, as well as explanations for their use in people's lives.

This leaves one other part of my thought process I want to share in regard to seeking advice. When you listen to someone's words of advice, take time to really evaluate the person's actions and figure out if they're giving you their honest life-changing counsel or just venting in the moment. Also, continue to seek knowledge from the many great teachers of this world and find a connection—it's going to happen eventually, so might as well start the relationship early. This is imperative for growth, so be careful whom you ask for advice—do you know the origins from which their knowledge flows? Most people are what they mentally consume on a daily basis for nourishment, knowledge, or what they deem important for their own lives. Understand that what's important to another may not be important to you and vice versa, so choose carefully if you're in the need of guidance from another person.

Also, ask yourself if you need physical hands-on help or just a listener? Understand that there's nothing wrong with a good listener, but be wise when it comes to this interaction. When one person vents, it's a verbal manifested burden being applied outwardly in the direction of whomever is the recipient. In this case, the recipient must think, *Is this worthy of my attention or time? Is this a rhetorical, unresolvable problem? What's expected of me?* and lastly, *Why me?* Tread carefully when you ask for advice, because someone you choose without thinking it through might turn out to be a reflection of who you used to be—"birds of a feather." In this case, it would be the blind leading the blind; this is not to say this person is a bad person, but forward movement means letting the past go.

Know that some people, in the absence of the purposeful consumption of knowledge, are being misdirected or simply fooled within the clutter of their own circumstances. Either way, be polite and continue your search for the honest mentor, worthy of promoting spiritual advice and life-changing confirmations. What if a person is highly educated or endowed with years of experience? These may be signs of good prospects, but still be honest with yourself.

Are their actions indicative of their title? Is their character in direct proportion to their acquired knowledge? Are you absolutely ready to commit to the advice? If given exceptional inspirational or motivational problem-solving advice, will you abide by seeing it through? Know that most reactions, temperament, visual comprehension, and expressive understandings are a reflection of the knowledge within a person's mental storehouse. In other words, you tend to see or hear what you want to, so as to make yourself feel safe and comfortable. So humble yourself; not all advice is easy to digest. If you find that dealing with people for advice is cumbersome at best, seek professional advisors, spiritual or motivational, and stay close until you're strong enough to continue on your destined path.

Try to refrain from contact with scattered sensationalism like social media quotes or people who pretend to walk the path for the sake of making a profit. An example, if you're watching soap operas as a daily ritual, your views and opinions will become a reflection of the sensationalistic imagery you've allowed to manifest in your mind. Bottom line: don't rely on others' advice if they partake of the same ritual.

Some say it's just entertainment, but be careful not to allow drama, misdirection, and confusion to become embedded in your consciousness. Again, you're seeking advice, not misdirection. Similarly, if you're enchanted or programmed by talk shows, your mind could become saturated with the mindset of a judgmental host, spotlighting and critiquing other people's fears, issues, shortcomings, or weaknesses. Be careful not to partake in this or you'll turn out to be a part of condemnation. If this happens, how will you ever find the peace within proper advice, being as you'll feel judged in return?

Remember to seek from within, not from the falsehoods of the world. Let's say you only watch "reality" television, such as competitive physical challenges or relationship-seeking or even talent shows. Again, all this adds up to you becoming judgmental, and before you know it, you've allowed a distraction to make directional changes in your path, furthermore taken your attention off of yourself by the stimulation of mind-consuming interest. Give your mind peace from the stories or trials of other goal-seeking people and focus on your own ambitions or desired achievements.

Know that the more you allow a scripted media show to seduce you, the greater the chances are that you'll push your true goals and purposes to the back burner. If this happens, you've subconsciously produced a fable by analyzing other people's accomplishments or failures; be careful not to inadvertently fall into a state of denial by shedding light on others instead of on your God given path.

No matter what your situation, if you have breath in your body, you have purpose. If you're elderly, write a book about your journey, failures, and successes. If you're young, speak out about your goals and read the books of the wise to see what to avoid and what to grab onto. We all have a purpose, but before most can achieve, they must have a catalyst of knowledge or advice that can point them into the right direction. So to know where to get this advice, you must evaluate your true self, purpose, and path. In doing this you hold yourself accountable for the entirety of the process. Ask yourself, "Am I ready to hear the truth?" If so, then face it and commit your whole self to follow through, no matter how difficult the challenge. And remember proper advice should lead to positive resolve.

Be aware, some people give outright bad advice because it's their best advice; when you notice this happening, consider why are you soliciting help or problem solving advice from a person who's drowning in their own unresolved problematic situations. In conclusion, and as stated before, hold yourself accountable when seeking advice; you wouldn't go to a dentist if you were in need of an enema, would you? Both professions are in fact professionals but one who fixes cavities and the other whom administers enemas are experts in their field, yet their tools of trade may not fit your purpose; literally speaking.

Even though I didn't go into full detail about my personal barriers in life, know that the specificity of this too will come in future works.

Let's just say that I'm sure a few of the issues I've dealt with, you or someone you know have dealt with as well. So, if you've overcome as many issues as I have or are currently going through them, hang in there, please! Your circumstances will surely get better. Besides, the ability to overcome is one of our many powers, remember?

However, if you're still curious to know some of the strongholds I've endured, surpassed, and conquered, I'll share some examples. Also, just so you'll know, while going through the many issues and strongholds placed upon my journey, that is from a small stones to the enormous boulders, I didn't indulge in any outlets like adultery, medication, projected defamation of character, or alcohol, narcotics or the like thereof. In other words, I faced all issues head-on. It took some time, as often I wasn't prepared, but the end result was triumphant and purpose finding, thanks to spiritual guidance.

For starters, you already know one of my earliest not-so-great memories, concerning my parents' sudden divorce. This was only the beginning of what can best be described as an all-out attack on a seven-year-old boy's purpose-driven life. What followed the divorce was an abrupt relocation of environment with Mom's new husband. Not only was it difficult to cope with moving from a house to an apartment, but my new stepfather was of a different nationality and he had no tolerance for us or our cultural understandings.

Soon after, within going back and forth between parents and babysitters came confusion, verbal abuse, physical abuse, sexual abuse and molestation, demonization of choosing between parents, custody battles, about five different grammar schools, three summer schools and three high schools; so being bullied was the norm, imagine almost every year in school being beaten, harassed and chased as the new and poor kid! Yep, there's more! Then comes staying with my grandparents and or temporary friends or families.

My father married five times, and my mother four times. I went back and forth, living within all their relationships, good or bad. By a certain point in my life, it wouldn't seem like I'd be a good prospect for anything worthwhile, but God works in miraculous ways.

Even still, there was more to come in the form of abandonment, embarrassment, poverty, and fear. By now, as life would have it I was getting older and tougher, so running away became a part of my life. In short, the decisions to run briefly turned into avoiding anything that required commitment. Afterward came early fatherhood, my first marriage, drug abuse, alcohol addiction, AAA classes and domestic violence. By now manifested seeds had started to arrive in response to my need, but still the notion that "life is a beast" had more to offer—such as job loss, my second child, fighting drug dealers from taking over my home, racism at work, adultery at home, being stabbed multiples times on different occasions, poverty, welfare, and soup kitchens, not to mention getting shot not once but twice on two other occasions within my struggle.

No problem—I was forged in the fire, right? Even still, I struggled along: third child, home evictions not once but twice, car impounded, car totaled, living in the projects, and then there was my divorce—hang in there, it'll all be over soon—engine blown, suspended driver's license, dropping out of high school, and failing the GED test not once but three times! Then came dropping out of college, paying child support, paying alimony, paying for others' court costs, having no transportation, suicidal thoughts, dealing with low self-esteem as well as depression, hunger, living on the streets, living in my van, a pseudo-relationship where I was more a prostitute than a boyfriend, working two jobs but being bankrupt, an unbelievably mind-boggling negative credit report, hypertension, anxiety attacks, high cholesterol, pericarditis of the heart, acid reflux, and anger issues.

I'll stop there because, truth is we all have or have had some form of these issues in our lives, the difference in my life is *I knew I had something to do* and I couldn't be the only one. Also, if I just kept moving forward, I would one day be able to help someone else get through what I was currently battling. Of course, looking back, I wouldn't trade what I've been through, not one bit! Now in the second phase of my life, as I said prior "I love, being in love!" I can actually say I'm loving it tremendously! The first half may not have been great, but as I noted a few times already, commitment, for no other reason and by way of the Holy Spirit, is the point. Besides, one of my hidden powers is to do battle and heal—in other words, to "overcome," same as yours, so complaining is ill-advised and it really wouldn't sit well in your spirit.

Now that I have vented a bit about my trials and experiences, I can't wait to tell you about my many successes, but that's a little later as we establish our connection. Know that in between all my failures was the strength to climb out of each pitfall. Also don't forget the encouragement of the biblical dreams and visions that opened up throughout my struggles. It's a good deed to witness, surviving through the darkness of the mind to see the enlightenment within the world. As said, I love life, and life's worth living diligently until you get it right. Also, know I hold much love for you in my heart, and by now you should know my words are not camouflaged as to insult anyone's intelligence. Rather, my words are open so you can see, feel, and acknowledge my journey. Accept that we're all survivors with a distinct purpose and destiny. We witness to become stronger, we connect to go farther, and we survive to rise higher. Thanks for spending time with me and taking on some of my prior issues from adolescence to adulthood. Know that it's reciprocal in all the love I can share.

Furthermore, the purpose of this book is to call to action all who have been exposed to a higher level of consciousness within the spirit. We have been endowed with a blessed responsibility, not a burden. Please accept that we are as one within this journey! Take hold of the lights of your gifts to elevate the positive essence of life as it was meant to be. In this time, in this reality, and as a part of this universe. Let's unite and fulfill our hearts' desires as we rise together. Cleanse your consciousness and release the weight of embedded misdirections.

You have all within your reach, you are well equipped, and are more than ready; take the journey. It's simple: we were created with infinite powers, and amongst these powers are the freedoms of choice and will.

Please refrain from the conformity of fear and misguided fallacies. In this you will encompass your inheritance of God's intended purpose for your life: that is for you to flourish in the abundance. Accept your responsibility and stay encouraged, for you were created for this specific task. Hold your powers firm and channel your positive vibration to that of a higher consciousness. Remember: if we've fallen in mind, body, or soul, it's only to make us stronger.

Lastly, no matter what state of mind you currently hold acknowledge you have an important role within the fabric of life. If at any time your weak, confused or exhausted not fully understanding your purpose, take a leap of faith and praise God anyway. Then raise your head while standing your ground, choose confidently that abundance is yours as you place one foot in front of the other and continue on your journey. This is the truth within your destiny and the purpose of your creation. Awaken my friends, dust off your worldly image! You are perfect within the creation of life, rise as the higher humans intricately weaved within the fabric of mankind.

Thank You.

THE CONSCIOUSNESS OF MAN

"In the absence of conformity, lies a place for great blessings."

-Reginald O'Neal Gibson

Personal Note

This book has been given unto you with love, peace, and admiration.

To: _____

From: _____

Let this signify a start to a wonderful journey; may God continually bless you.

Date: _____

Special thanks to

DONALD JAMES GIBSON JR.

My son REGINALD GIBSON,

PETER ANTHONY WARTINGER

ANTHONY ROMAN WARTINGER

EMMANEUL J. MOOTY

&

TIMOTHY

THE CONSCIOUSNESS OF MAN

COMING SOON!

THE CONSCIOUSNESS OF MAN;

Analogies revealed

www.ingramcontent.com/pod-product-compliance
Lightning Source LLC
Chambersburg PA
CBHW032045150426
43194CB00006B/423